GW00371008

Smash!

Jack Rosenthal

A SAMUEL FRENCH ACTING EDITION

SAMUEL FRENCH
FOUNDED 1830

SAMUELFRENCH.COM
SAMUELFRENCH-LONDON.CO.UK

ISBN 978 0 573 11390 1

www.SamuelFrench.com
www.SamuelFrench-London.co.uk

FOR PRODUCTION ENQUIRIES

Plays@SamuelFrench-London.co.uk
020-7255-4302/01

The Professional Rights in this play are controlled by CASAROTTO RAMSAY AND ASSOCIATES, 7-12 NOEL STREET, LONDON, W1F 8GQ

Each title is subject to availability from Samuel French, depending upon country of performance. Please be aware that *SMASH!* may not be licensed by Samuel French in your territory. Producers should contact the nearest Samuel French office or licensing partner to verify availability.

SMASH! was first performed at the Cambridge Arts Theatre in May 1981. The performance was directed by Barry Davis and Jonathan Lynn, designed by Robin Archer with costumes by Rob Ringwood, lighting by Andrew Bridge and music composed and realised by Ray Cook. The cast was as follows:

LIZ .... Maureen Lipman

THEO .... Nigel Hawthorne

STACEY ....Stephen Moore

MIKE .... Peter Blake

BEBE .... Larry Adler

Additional roles played by Sue Burton, Jean Rimmer and Vincenzo Nicoli.

This was followed by a tour in which Bebe was played by John Bluthall.

SMASH! was revived at the Menier Chocolate Factory, London, in March 2011. The performance was directed by Tamara Harvey, designed by Paul Farnsworth with lighting by Tim Mitchell, sound by Gareth Owen and additional material supplied by Amy Rosenthal. The cast was as follows:

LIZ ....Natalie Walter

THEO ....Tom Conti

STACEY .... Cameron Blakely

MIKE ....Josh Cohen

BEBE ....Richard Schiff

Additional roles played by Carrie Quinlan and Sam Parks

CHARACTERS

LIZ – An English novelist in her early 30s
THEO – An American producer of European origin In his early 60s
STACEY – An American director About 40
MIKE – An English lyric-writer. Mid 30s
BEBE – An American composer in his 60s
FEMALE DANCER
WAITRESS
D.J. (VOICE ONLY)
BOARD OPERATOR (ELECTRICIAN)
WAITER

SETTING

Various simple interior settings in New York, Manchester and London.

TIME

1980s

ACT ONE

(A suite in a swanky New York hotel. An evening in June, about 8 p.m.)

*(**THEO** is unpacking an expensive suitcase, singing happily as he slings clothes onto the backs of chairs or hangs suits in the wardrobe (offstage L). He's straight from the shower and wearing an exotic dressing gown.)*

(SR is a trolley from Room Service. On it is a generous and tempting buffet supper for five.)

(There's a knock offstage R.)

THEO. If that's the best author in the world, you can come in. Anyone else – go screw yourself.

*(Offstage R sounds of door opening. **LIZ** enters. She's a little dishevelled, travel-weary and struggling to keep awake. She carries a script in her bag. **THEO** throws her a glance – and grins.)*

I'm never wrong – the best author in the world!

LIZ. Thank Christ for that. For one tantalising minute I wasn't sure whether to go away and screw myself.

THEO. I love her, I love her, every word a gem, come in, sit down, I love her. There's tea, coffee, black, white, lemon, cream, whatever your heart desires. Sandwiches, apple strudel, English muffins.

LIZ. English muffins?

THEO. You bet English muffins.

LIZ. In New York New York?

THEO. Where else? You ever see an English muffin in England England?

LIZ. Well, not since I was five. And then it was only in Enid Blyton.

(She goes to the trolley and peers at its contents.)

LIZ. What do they look like?

THEO. Liz, don't give me a bad time about muffins. Eat, enjoy and say thank you – or sit down and forget it. You're hungry – go bite your nails.

LIZ. I only wanted to know what they look like.

THEO. The most exciting night of your life – and you get a confectionery fixation! Have apple strudel instead.

LIZ. I was only trying to <u>identify</u> them. I'm the best author in the world – I'm supposed to have an inquisitive mind. Not so easy when one of your eyelids keeps falling down...

*(**THEO** storms irritably to the trolley. He slaps a sandwich onto a plate and thrusts it into her hands.)*

THEO. Nah! Cheese sandwich. American cheese. From Switzerland. Eat.

LIZ. I will. I will. I'll have a word with my jawbone and see how it feels about going up and down.

*(She yawns helplessly, puts the plate back on the trolley and pours herself a coffee. After a moment, **THEO** turns, smiles at her, triumphantly.)*

THEO. Well, young woman. I promised you New York. You got it.

LIZ. Thank you. It's very nice.

THEO. Excited?

LIZ. I think I've got jet-lag.

THEO. "Excited? I think I got jet-lag"! That was me sitting next to you on the plane! Have <u>I</u> got jet-lag?

LIZ. You <u>slept</u> all the way!

THEO. Liz, for Chrissakes! You want to give me a pacemaker for my birthday? You're in the most exciting city in the world! Look out the window! You got such beautiful skyscrapers in Wimbledon?

LIZ. Theo, don't get —

THEO. You got the Chrysler Building at the end of your block in Wimbledon?

LIZ. Look, all I'm —

THEO. Don't be such a Little Englander!

LIZ. Why are you shouting so much?

THEO. Why are giving me such a bad time?

LIZ. You didn't shout like that in London.

THEO. Here it don't mean nothing. *(a beat)* It just indicates you're in show-business.

LIZ. So what about the cab driver? He shouted at us all the way from Kennedy Airport.

THEO. This is America – <u>everybody's</u> in show-business. That's why you're here.

*(Suddenly the air is split by an approaching ambulance siren. It reaches its terrifying crescendo as the ambulance passes the hotel, then gradually fades away. **LIZ** is staring at the window in horror.)*

LIZ. What the hell's that? Evensong?

*(**THEO** ignores her. He continues unpacking. Offended. Martyred. And making sure **LIZ** notices so she can feel guilty. She sighs.)*

Alright, Theo, I'll work on it. Tomorrow I'll have a nice walk down Fourth Avenue —

THEO. <u>Fifth</u> Avenue.

LIZ. ...Fifth Avenue, and be excited. But <u>tonight</u> I can make no promises for. In that, so far, all I've seen of —

THEO. Fourth Avenue! Who goes down Fourth Avenue?

LIZ. In that, so far, all I've seen of New York is the Customs Shed at the airport, a cab ride at eighty miles an hour with no springs, and an English muffin.

THEO. <u>Again</u> with her English muffins!

LIZ. I'm sorry, Theo. I'm bombed. My brain keeps sliding about. If I could just sleep for three days...

THEO. Tomorrow you can sleep for three days – between breakfast and lunch. Fifth Avenue can take it – Fourth

Avenue even – <u>tonight</u>, however, you keep awake.
That's an official order from your producer.

LIZ. Incidentally, Theo, when the hell am I getting a
contract? According to my agent —

THEO. Wonderful woman, your agent, the best. You keep
awake. And happy. And <u>excited</u>. In five minutes they'll
be here. <u>They'll</u> be excited. You'll have the most
exciting night of your life. Did I ever tell you a lie?

LIZ. Do they like the script?

THEO. Listen – the best author in the world – they love it!

LIZ. Did they <u>say</u> so?

THEO. I'm the producer – <u>I</u> said so. It's perfect. They <u>said</u>
so.

LIZ. Good. They're not just <u>saying</u> so?

THEO. To <u>death</u> they love it! Listen, jet-lag I accept. Being a
wet-blanket I accept. You're English – it's natural. But
if you're going to make like a sensitive writer all night
– "Do they love it? Did they say so? Will they swear on a
stack of whatisits...?"

LIZ. Bibles.

THEO. "Bibles" ...then, young woman, you get a king-size
kick in the ass, OK? Nine hundred dollars it cost me
to get you here, and that don't include the five dollars
seventy-five for the headphones so's you could watch
California Suite!

LIZ. They didn't work. One side kept slipping out of my
ear.

THEO. A Neil Simon movie. You should've listened with
the other ear. You might've learnt how to write a <u>half</u>
decent script!

LIZ. *(alarmed)* I thought you said they loved it?

THEO. I'm joking, for Chrissake, I'm joking!!

LIZ. Sorry.

(A pause. THEO *carries his suitcase offstage L)*

THEO. You unpacked your case?

LIZ. Half of it. Till I realised Jim'd forgotten to pack my face flannel. Then I lost interest. So then I just lay on the bed, trying to understand the cartoons in the *New Yorker.*

THEO. *(offstage)* You took a shower?

LIZ. What – with no face flannel? I'm English!

*(***THEO*** angrily re-enters L)*

*(Glares at ***LIZ***)*

LIZ. *(imitating ***THEO***'s accent)* I'm joking, for Chrissake, I'm joking! I had a nice English bath and a pot of tea – with a tea bag in it – made me all nice and ready for bed. It's two o'clock in the morning my time, Theo.

THEO. Liz. Please. Enough. Please stop...stop doing whatever it is you're doing... Being so...so... Try and liven up a little!

LIZ. Tell you what I'll do. What I'll do is try and liven up a little. In fact, seeing it's you and it's cost you nine hundred and five dollars seventy-five cents to get me here, I'll even start getting excited. This is me getting excited, alright?

(She beams a broad, fixed grin at him. He sighs.)

*(The phone rings. ***THEO*** grabs it)*

THEO. Thank you. Would you send him right up please? Thank you.

*(He replaces the phone. Turns to ***LIZ*** and smiles triumphantly.)*

Well, he's here. The great man. The greatest. In person. In the flesh. In the lobby.

*(Despite her Englishness, her jet-lag and herself, ***LIZ*** is now excited. She looks at ***THEO***. Tenses.)*

LIZ. Bebe Kaiser?

*(***THEO*** smiles at her. Smugly. Modestly.)*

THEO. We sat in Grosvenor Square, you and I, right? We had with us our lyric writer, the best in England, whatshisname?

LIZ. Mike.

THEO. Mike! And I made you a promise. "Give me your novel *Whatever Happened to Tomorrow?* to turn into a musical – and I'll give you the greatest of them all to write the score". Well, Miss Lizzie, promises I <u>keep</u>. So sue me. I promised you absolutely the best composer in the world – you got him.

(There's a knock at the door (offstage R))

LIZ. Also absolutely the fastest. How's he got up fifteen floors in three point two seconds?

*(*THEO *exits R)*

THEO. *(offstage)* Bebe! Sonofabitch!

(Sound of door opening)

STACEY. *(entering R)* Or even <u>Stacey</u>-sonofabitch!

THEO. *(entering R)* *(puzzled)* Stacey-baby! The desk-clerk said that Bebe was —

STACEY. Liz! You made it!

(He strides across to her, smiling, arms extended. She meets him more than half-way. They hug each other delightedly.)

*(*LIZ *pulls away – a little quicker than she'd like to. A little embarrassedly.)*

It's wonderful to see you again!

LIZ. *(laughing)* You, too!

STACEY. Welcome to civilization!

LIZ. If you say so.

THEO. Stacey. According to the desk-clerk...

STACEY. *(to* LIZ*)* You're looking terrific!

LIZ. I've been travelling all day!

STACEY. For someone who's been travelling all day – you look more than terrific!

LIZ. Well, you don't look too lousy yourself...

THEO. Stacey, did you see Bebe in the lobby?

STACEY. Theo, I don't see nobody in lobbies. I don't even see <u>lobbies</u>. I want to go to a room, I catch the elevator and go to the room. The job satisfaction of desk-clerks isn't too high on my list of priorities, OK? *(to* **LIZ***)* So how are you?

LIZ. Tired.

THEO. But <u>happy</u>. She's tired but happy.

STACEY. Terrific.

(He smiles at her.)

STACEY. Well, Miss Morris, the big day's arrived.

LIZ. This is it.

STACEY. Day one.

LIZ. Day one.

STACEY. Hey, what date is it, anyway? We should make a note of the date, then a year from now we'll be able to —

THEO. Twenty-fifth of June. I know it's the twenty-fifth of June, tomorrow's my birthday. And my birthday's the twenty-sixth. As a producer it pays to know these things.

STACEY. *(to* **LIZ***)(half smiling, half solemn)* June twenty-fifth next year, my girl, you'll be the only — what's the word for a citizen of Wimbledon?

LIZ. I don't know. A womble.

STACEY. Well, whatever, you'll be the only one of them driving three Rolls Royces. Maybe four. The toast of the West End. The year <u>after</u> – the toast of Broadway. You'll get free luncheon vouchers at Sardi's. For life. We've got a hit.

LIZ. *(laughs)* That's the second-nicest thing anyone's ever said to me...

STACEY. More than a hit – a <u>smash</u>.

THEO. Wait. When we make the show we got a hit. Till then all we got is a...a something hit. A whatyoucallit. There's a word for it.

LIZ. "Possible"?

THEO. "Potential". We got a <u>potential</u> hit.

STACEY. Theo, trust me. I can smell a smash <u>two</u> Atlantics away.

*(He takes **LIZ**'s hands in his.)*

The first draft's terrific. Terrific.

THEO. See! What'd I tell you!

LIZ. Thank you, Stacey.

STACEY. For a first draft, we're in business.

THEO. *(to **LIZ**)* Alright? Satisfied? OK, now do <u>me</u> a favour. Get excited.

LIZ. *(to **STACEY**)* I'll pour you a coffee.

STACEY. <u>Theo</u> pours the coffee. He's the producer. That's his job.

THEO. My own fault. I'm dumb enough to hire me absolutely the best director on Broadway. I get insults.

(He goes happily over to the trolley to pour coffee.)

LIZ. Sure you don't want me to do it, Theo?

THEO. Sit. Sit. You're a whatisit celebrity. Potential.

(He pours coffee.)

*(**STACEY** sprawls in the chair L. As **LIZ** goes to sit on sofa:)*

STACEY. I don't suppose you had time to ring Harrods for me, Liz? See if they could get me the vicuna gloves?

LIZ. Last Monday.

STACEY. *(excited)* You did?

LIZ. I told them you'd be back in London in three weeks and would they have them by then? An hour later they delivered them to Wimbledon. Chauffeur-driven vicuna gloves.

STACEY. You <u>got</u> them? Good girl.

LIZ. *(as delighted as he is)* I brought them with me. In my bag.

STACEY. All that trouble! You're a doll!

LIZ. What trouble? It was no trouble. I enjoyed it. They weren't heavy.

*(She hands package to **STACEY**)*

STACEY. Thank you.

LIZ. My pleasure.

(The line is said with a sudden tender smile. She at once turns it into the safety of a grin.)

Not at all.

THEO. *(coffee cup in hand)* What to eat Stacey? *(he looks back at trolley)* I got cheese, ham –

LIZ. *(taking coffee cup and handing to **STACEY**)* Which hotel are you at?

STACEY. Hotel? My apartment.

LIZ. Oh, of course.

*(**THEO** glances from one to the other, puzzled.)*

THEO. He <u>lives</u> here in New York.

*(**LIZ** is suddenly embarrassed. She laughs her way quickly out of it.)*

LIZ. I know. I know. He's always in <u>hotels</u>. I just wondered which <u>hotel</u> he was in. *(to **THEO**)* He's not in a hotel. He lives here. Forget it. Jet-lag.

*(**LIZ** sits on sofa, **THEO** crosses to the trolley.)*

THEO. I got cheese, ham, egg and tomato, apple strudel. You name it. Don't name caviar. That waits for opening night.

STACEY. I've just had six jumbo prawn cocktails.

THEO. Six?? You're a greedy bastard.

STACEY. For lunch I had seven.

THEO. *(to* **LIZ***)* <u>Everybody's</u> a character in New York. You'll notice that.

LIZ. *(to* **STACEY***)* So you really, really like it, then? <u>Really</u>?

THEO. Well, if he had <u>seven</u> for lunch, for Chrissake!

LIZ. No – the script, the first draft.

(*There's a knock at the door (offstage R)*)

THEO. Bebe!

(**THEO** *exits R*)

LIZ. *(to* **STACEY***)* Do I curtsey or go on my knees?

STACEY. Don't let him intimidate you. Just treat him like any ordinary legend-in-his-own-lifetime.

THEO. *(offstage)* Jesus Christ — where's Bebe?

MIKE. *(entering R)* Evening all.

(**MIKE** *stops, grins at* **LIZ**, *arms outstretched.*)

MIKE. There's the girl!

LIZ. There's the feller!

(*They stand and hug each other*)

THEO. Mike – did you see Bebe in the lobby?

MIKE. *(to* **LIZ***)* So what's the news from home?

LIZ. When did you leave?

MIKE. Friday.

LIZ. Middlesex were 63 for 5. Brearley got a duck.

MIKE. Shows you. I can't turn my back for two minutes.

(*He turns to* **STACEY**)

Hello, mate.

(*He fishes a cigarette lighter from his pocket.*)

Stacey, you left your lighter in the Russian Tea Rooms, lunchtime.

(*He throws lighter to* **STACEY**)

STACEY. Thanks, Mike.

MIKE. *(to* **LIZ***)* How's Jim?

LIZ. Oh, fine. Looking forward to fish and chips for every meal while I'm away. How's Valerie and the kids?

MIKE. Ugh, who cares? I ring them thirty-six times a day in case they hadn't noticed I'd gone. *(a beat)* They hadn't. Did you have a good flight?

THEO. Mike. Liz. Do me a favour... Tomorrow you can discuss turbulence, OK? Tonight, however, is tonight. Tonight we all meet up again. Official. *Variety* did half a column on that very fact. How come they knew? Because I told them – mine was the only name they spelt wrong. That, I also told them. So please, Mike, when I ask you a question you answer. Number one: did you eat yet? Number two: would you like a pickle? and number three: <u>what</u> <u>in</u> <u>the</u> <u>hell</u> <u>happened</u> <u>to</u> <u>Bebe?</u>

MIKE. *(to LIZ)* So have they told you the good news?

LIZ. Mmm? Sorry, I was listening to this gentleman.

MIKE. The first draft. *Whatever Happened to Tomorrow?* Has Stacey told you?

LIZ. *(grins)* He likes it.

STACEY. He <u>loves</u> it. It's terrific. She knows. A little potchkeying here and there, maybe. Nothing.

THEO. *(to MIKE)* Excuse me...

LIZ. *(to MIKE)* Do you like it?

MIKE. I think it's tremendous, Liz.

THEO. *(to MIKE)* Excuse me...

MIKE. *(to LIZ)* I already rang Valerie and told <u>her</u>. Perhaps <u>she'll</u> ring <u>Jim</u>.

THEO. *(to MIKE)* Excuse me...

MIKE. *(to LIZ)* I read it twice yesterday morning when I got it. Again in the afternoon. Again in bed last night. I think it's the most —

THEO. *(at the top of his voice)* Hey! Absolutely the best lyric writer in the world – who's the shitface producer round here?!

(A small pause)

MIKE. You are, Theo.

THEO. Thank you.

(*Unseen by* **THEO**, *the others share schoolboy grins.*)

Now, the desk-clerk calls me up. "Mr. Bebe Kaiser is in the lobby." A sentence like that no one makes up for the hell of it. So all I want to know —

MIKE. He <u>was</u> in the lobby. We both were. We're standing there waiting for the lift – and guess who comes flouncing out?

THEO. Mike, we have to play guessing games? I been on an airplane for eight hours!

MIKE. Liza Minelli!

THEO. Liza!

STACEY. Liza in town? I bumped into her in LA two weeks ago. She was eating lobster for breakfast in the Beverley Wilshire. For <u>breakfast</u>, yet. Me – I had jumbo prawn cocktail. Three.

MIKE. So. She sees Bebe. He sees her. And they stand there kissing and canoodling and talking about dental floss!

THEO. So what. <u>I</u> talked to her about dental floss plenty times.

MIKE. And I'm standing there like someone who's never actually going to be introduced – so the lift came – so I took it. Anyway, that's where he is. (*A beat. Then to* **THEO**) What <u>sort</u> of pickle?

THEO. (*puzzled*) Pickle?

MIKE. You offered me a pickle.

THEO. So take one! How do <u>I</u> know what sort? They're pickles. I didn't know they <u>came</u> in sorts.

MIKE. A nice cup of tea, then, no sugar. How's that?

(**THEO** *goes to pour tea.*)

(*to* **LIZ**) So there I was in bed reading your first draft. Need I say more – I had fourteen black lesbians in there with me – and I didn't even give them a second glance.

LIZ. You decided to stick at the basic fourteen?

MIKE. Well, New York, I'm snookered. Ealing's a different proposition. In Ealing I've got that much larger a circle of black lesbian friends. Then this morning I rang Stacey and told him it's the best first draft I've ever read.

STACEY. And I told him the same.

THEO. Me too.

MIKE. Him too.

(Another ambulance ear-splittingly sirens its way past the hotel, drowning out the last three lines.)

LIZ. What the hell <u>are</u> they? Police cars?

STACEY. Ambulances.

LIZ. With <u>patients</u> inside? Don't they die of fright?

STACEY. They don't hear. By the time they reach the hospital they're stone deaf. Permanently.

*(**STACEY** takes a diary from his bag.)*

STACEY. Theo, while we're waiting. You want to fix the production schedules Manchester and London?

THEO. Not till Bebe gets here. Dates and times we do together. You're talking to an experienced producer.

MIKE. What time is it now? Nine?

STACEY. Five after.

MIKE. I'll ring home. Alright to use your phone, Theo?

THEO. In Ealing it's two a.m.

MIKE. I'll pay for the call.

THEO. Who's arguing dollars? I'll pay for <u>ten</u> calls. You want to wake whatshername up at two a.m.?

(A beat.)

MIKE. I'll call her first thing in the morning.

THEO. Call her first thing in the morning.

*(There's a knock at the door (Offstage R) **THEO** exits R)*

LIZ. Legend in his own lifetime. Legend in his own lifetime.

THEO. *(offstage)* Bebe! Sonofabitch! You look wonderful!

(BEBE strides briskly in, wearing hat and jacket. (They remain on throughout the scene.) **THEO** *follows.)*

BEBE. So, for twenty dollars, who do I bump into in the lobby, you won't believe! *(to MIKE)* So what in the hell happened to you? One minute you're there; the next, pure oxygen. I could've introduced you. Does no harm a British lyric writer meeting someone like her. *(to STACEY)* I bumped into an old friend of yours. For twenty dollars. Guess.

STACEY. I heard. I heard.

BEBE. Oh, you heard. So don't guess. At today's prices, twenty bucks is twenty bucks.

STACEY. How is she?

BEBE. She's a star, that's how she is. I love her to death. That doesn't stop her being a small pain in the ass, but how often do I see her? *(to THEO)* You got coffee there?

(BEBE sits in armchair R)

THEO. Everything. For the best, I get the best of everything. Flown in.

BEBE. Small coffee, two sugars, no cream.

(As THEO goes to pour coffee, MIKE points at LIZ and BEBE.)

THEO. *(to MIKE)* You want to phone, <u>phone</u>! Don't give me looks! *(to BEBE)* For "moon" and "June" I gotta jump through hoops? *(a beat)* So. At last. Here we are. Day one.

LIZ. Ahem!

THEO. Speaking as the producer, it gives me great honour —

MIKE. Theo? Are you going to introduce Liz and Bebe to each other?

THEO. Excuse me?

MIKE. You haven't introduced them.

THEO. Oh my God – Bebe, Liz, I apologise! I had this crazy idea the whole team had already —

LIZ. Everyone except Mr. Kaiser and me.

THEO. Bebe, allow me. This is your author, Liz. Liz – your esteemed composer, the one and only Bebe Kaiser!

LIZ. *(offering her hand to be shaken)* I'm honoured to meet you, Mr. Kaiser.

(BEBE doesn't look at her. He sits staring ahead. A silence.)

(The others exchange uncomfortable looks.)

LIZ. I'm very pleased to make your acquaintance, Mr. Kaiser.

BEBE. Liza wants me to write the music for her next movie. She also asked if I had any dental floss. Imagine, a star like that, she'd run out of dental floss!

(An uncomfortable silence. MIKE clears his throat.)

(LIZ looks to STACEY for help.)

STACEY. Bebe. This is Liz. She said she was pleased to meet you.

BEBE. Yeah? That pleases her, does it? Well, fine, I'll roast a turkey, we'll have a parade! You know what'd please me? Knowing how to put flesh and blood into those cardboard asshole characters of hers! She got any ideas? 'Cause sure as hell I aint!

(He sits staring ahead in prickly silence. The others – in embarrassment.)

THEO. Bebe...Stacey was impatient we talk schedules. The way I figured, we could all meet up in London round about —

LIZ. What exactly do you mean, Mr. Kaiser?

STACEY. Before London, Theo. Mike can work with Bebe here. Meantime, I steer Liz through another couple of drafts —

LIZ. *(to BEBE)* What cardboard characters?

THEO. OK, Liz, cool it! We're here to discuss like rational human beings, OK? You want violence, get the elevator, there's a streetful of it down there...

LIZ. I don't believe what's happening!

MIKE. Bebe...

LIZ. No, Mike, I'm here. He can talk to me. Mr. Kaiser, if you'd kindly... I'd very much appreciate... I'd...

(Bewildered and angry, she looks to STACEY for support. He frowns and shakes his head, indicating that she should let the moment go.)

STACEY. What I'm proposing is, by mid-November, early December, we should be sitting on all our basic musical numbers and our rehearsal script.

(STACEY's speech gathers speed. LIZ stares at him, throughout. To her – and us – it's almost incomprehensible.)

Meantime Theo, I'll have approved the set designs and models —

BEBE. Yeah, well have yourselves a ball, fellers, sorry I won't be with you.

(A stunned silence. THEO fidgets.)

THEO. Bebe...Bebe-baby... You called me in London last week. You said you and Mike already had two numbers worked out – ideas for two numbers – to put in the show —

BEBE. If I was doing the show, sure. I'd be glad to.

(THEO looks at the others. They look back at him.)

THEO. You are doing the show!

BEBE. With no script?

STACEY. OK, Bebe, simmer down.

(BEBE leaps ferociously to his feet.)

BEBE. "Simmer down"? I need a a smart-ass with a scarf down to his ankles to tell me to simmer down? I'm down, Mac. Right down. Where I've been all day.

THEO. *(gently)* Bebe. You got the script yesterday. Special messenger. Hand-<u>delivered</u>. The first draft.

BEBE. Oh, I see! So that's what it was?

LIZ. Mr. Kaiser, would you care to tell us what you don't like about it? Would that be a start?

BEBE. Theo, we ain't had the privilege of previously working together, you don't know my nature. Now you're seeing my nature. My nature is to be helpful. I'll give you a for-instance. You now need a topline composer to take my place, right? I can name you a dozen. For a guy who's hit Broadway as many times as <u>I</u> have —

THEO. You're the best. Absolutely the best. Haven't I always said so? Hand on heart.

BEBE. Melodically – Julie Styne's the best. Dramatically – Steve Sondheim is the best. If you like that kind of thing. Other people say I'm the best. Well, that's not for me to say. Twenty-eight Broadway shows, so what's a shmock like me know? Twenty-eight Broadway smasheroos. *(to **STACEY**)* How many <u>you</u> done? Two? Three? So that gives you the right under the Constitution to wear a scarf down to your ankles and tell me to simmer down? <u>I</u> <u>did</u> <u>not</u> <u>get</u> <u>no</u> <u>first</u> <u>draft</u> <u>delivered</u>! I got a fancy packet of <u>crap</u> delivered!

(A helpless silence)

THEO. Well, that's what we're here for... *(small pause)*. To exchange points of view... *(small pause)* Speaking as the producer...

BEBE. Speaking as the producer, you get off your ass, get on that phone, call anyone who's got a goddamn pen — in New York, in LA, in Dayton-goddamn-Ohio — and get a goddamn script written! This broad here, she wrote a nice little novel, I know that. You go in a library in London, it's on the shelf. She won prizes for it. Fine. She now turns it into a script for a musical. She gets no prizes from me. I got nothing further to say.

(A silence)

MIKE. Anybody fancy a pickle?

(He gets no response to his question.)

THEO. Bebe, she's written seven novels, seven <u>famous</u> novels.

LIZ. Three, actually.

THEO. Three. Same thing!

STACEY. *(sighing)* Bebe. We've both been in this business long enough to know that —

BEBE. I got nothing further to say, Golden Boy. You just stand there and wear your scarf. In the middle of summer.

STACEY. It's a first draft for Chrissake!

MIKE. No one's denying that...here and there bits of it might need...

STACEY. There's time, Bebe, there's time. Liz here, she'll hammer out <u>six</u> more drafts before we're in rehearsal. This is the <u>first</u>.

*(**BEBE** turns to **LIZ** for the first time.)*

BEBE. You'd like to discuss what's wrong, right? A discussion.

*(**THEO** moves **LIZ** nearer to **BEBE**)*

I'll try and help you out. Now hear this.

(He raps out his words with rapid intensity.)

You got no conflict. You got no real characters. You got no love-interest. You got no narrative drive. You got no climax. You don't even got a happy ending. All you got is "he says this, she says that". Words!

LIZ. *(to **THEO**)* Words, eh? The things these authors get up to...

BEBE. *(not even hearing her)* Thousands and thousands of words. And, in my bones, I don't feel one solitary song in any one of them. All you got is crap.

(A silence)

THEO. Nobody said the first draft was <u>perfect</u>.

LIZ. <u>You</u> did.

(Impasse. **MIKE** *suddenly goes to the phone and dials the operator.)*

MIKE. *(into phone)* Would you get me a call, please? To London, *(a beat)* London, <u>England</u>. *(a beat)* 579 8225. *(a beat)* Thank you.

STACEY. Liz?

LIZ. Mmm?

STACEY. Off the top of my head...

LIZ. Pardon?

STACEY. Coupla suggestions, OK?

LIZ. *(surprised)* Um...of course.

MIKE. *(into phone)* Thanks. You're welcome, *(beat)* Yes, thank you, <u>you're</u> welcome as well. *(beat)* I'm trying to have a nice day.

STACEY. *(rapidly)* You write a prologue preceding Scene One – two or three pages, tops. We cut all of Scene Four and half of Scene Five.

LIZ. Um...

MIKE. *(into phone)* Hello, Val? Me! Who else rings you at two in the morning? Are the kids alright?

STACEY. The stuff in Scene Five can go part in Scene Three, as is...

MIKE. *(into phone)* Did the decorator come? He said today, didn't he? Oh, yeah, that's right, it's still yesterday here...

STACEY. And the rest in a rewritten Scene Six.

LIZ. Um...

STACEY. Then you change Act One Scene Two...

BEBE. Liz, change nothing.

LIZ. *(thrown even more)* What – you <u>like</u> it now?

MIKE. *(into phone)* No, just a sort of friendly meeting...

BEBE. Theo, you want a musical with no music, stick to what she's written.

STACEY. *(losing temper and throwing script on the ground)* We're talking about a new draft, Bebe! By August first, Bebe! We are not talking about laundry lists, we're talking about artistic creativity!

MIKE. *(into phone)* Got anyone interesting in bed with you?

BEBE. Oh, artistic creativity! Well, why did no one say?

MIKE. *(into phone)* Three Japanese wrestlers and an Israeli hermaphrodite. Anyone I know?

BEBE. Now me, I've only done twenty-eight Broadway blockbusters, what the hell do I know about artistic creativity!

MIKE. *(into phone)* Well, I should turn the electric blanket down, love.

BEBE. Seventeen Hollywood movies, nine TV Specials, six appearances on the Ed Sullivan show...

STACEY. OK, Bebe, OK.

THEO. Just relax, Bebe. You're not a young man. *(a beat, then* THEO *realises what he has said)* I speak from a similar position.

*(*MIKE *makes "kisses" at the phone then replaces it. Everyone is looking at him.)*

MIKE. She didn't take a sleeping pill, specially.

(A silence. He puts down phone.)

STACEY. August first then, Liz, no problem?

LIZ. I suppose not. If you say not.

STACEY. The which I do. *(to* BEBE*)* The which means that you and Mike could start August second.

*(*MIKE, THEO *and* LIZ *all turn to look at* BEBE. *A pause.)*

BEBE. A show's gotta have conflict.

(All look to STACEY*)*

STACEY. We'll have conflict.

(All look to BEBE*)*

BEBE. Conflict is essential.

(*All look to* **STACEY**)

STACEY. Conflict there'll be.

(*All look to* **BEBE**)

BEBE. Without conflict you are dead.

(*All look to* **STACEY**)

STACEY. I promise you conflict.

(*All slow turn to* **BEBE** *for his decision. A tense pause.*)

BEBE. OK, let's get this goddamn show on the road.

(**BEBE** *sits. Everyone sags, washed in relief.* **STACEY** *picks up his script and sits L.* **MIKE** *helps* **LIZ** *and they both sit on sofa.*)

THEO. Gentlemen. <u>Lady</u> and gentlemen. I think I'm allowed to say a few well-chosen words. When I was six years old, I played hookey from kindergarten and took me to the Vienna State Opera House. Matinee. Mozart. The Marriage of Whatshisname. And since that time I been in showbusiness all my life. I've produced shows all over the world. Some of them, believe me, <u>out</u> of this world. Like this one, I hope, please God. And I've never yet known a show – and Bebe will correct me if I'm wrong – where there hasn't been some slight gentleman's disagreement over <u>something</u>.

(**THEO** *suddenly turns to* **MIKE**)

No let me finish!

MIKE. I never opened my mouth!

THEO. Do me that honour! Producers and royalty are allowed to finish – it's an unwritten law! Disagreements mean nothing. Except that we have the <u>show</u> at heart. We're all friends, all embarking on a great howd'youcallit. Liz and Bebe – fruitfully in my belief – have now come face to face and exchanged artistic points of view. We all have one common goal: to make a hit show. In the winter, we all meet up again in England. With a final script, wonderful score, a wonderful cast, please God, our choreographer, our sets under construction. Everything money can buy. And the money, my friends, we <u>have</u>! Half a million dollars <u>fully</u> subscribed by my investors. Every day *(to* **MIKE***)* ask my secretary – I got investors banging my door down – begging, <u>begging</u> to invest more. And why? Because – and here I speak with my producer's hat on – we got ourselves a hit – a whatisit hit —

LIZ. "Potential".

THEO. A potential hit. We got in this room – and I flatter no one when I say this because in showbusiness there's no such thing as flattery – we got in this room, the best composer bar none, the best director, the best lyricist. We'll work. We'll have fun. Er...someone I missed out – oh, yes, and the best <u>author</u>. We'll work, we'll have fun. And by this time next year, we'll have that hit. Now – there's tea, coffee, black, white, lemon, cream...

(The screaming clanging siren of another ambulance approaching drowns out his words)

Scene Two

(A rehearsal room in North London.)

(There's a piano with a cassette-recorder on top of it; a piano chair; three rickety chairs around a trestle table littered with pages of scripts, sheet music and dirty mugs and ashtrays. A smaller table SL has telephone, teapot, cups, spoons, etc. on it.)

(The cassette is playing the title song of the show – **"WHATEVER HAPPENED TO TOMORROW?"** *– played on a piano.)*

(A young female **DANCER** *is dancing to the music. She's wearing rehearsal dancing costume. She's very uncertain of her steps, her moves and the music.)*

(STACEY *strides on. He sees the* **DANCER** *then goes over to the cassette and switches it off.)*

STACEY. What time do you make it, Annabel?

(She looks at her watch)

DANCER. Um...ten past six, nearly, Mr. Caine.

STACEY. What time did I break you for the day, Annabel?

DANCER. Six, Mr. Caine.

STACEY. Thank you, Annabel. So what in hell are you doing here at nine <u>after</u>?

DANCER. *(cowed)* Well, what with the rush-hour, there's no point really in me going to the Tube till —

STACEY. I broke at six, Annabel. I broke at six because I've been breaking your fat asses since nine this morning. When I say work, you work: you rest when I say rest. Jesus! All day long I hear English accents beefing about how you're all dropping with exhaustion, what a slave-driver I am, should you ring Equity! Now get your butt outa here with the other donkeys, OK? See you in the morning, g'bye!

DANCER. No, the point is really, that, what with the rush-hour —

STACEY. G'bye, Annabel! And take your pianist with you!

(He slings the cassette at her. She catches it.)

DANCER. It belongs to the Production Office, Mr. Caine.

STACEY. Here!

(He indicates she throw it back to him. She does so. He catches it and puts it on the table.)

G'bye!

DANCER. Mr. Caine, I was only trying to —

STACEY. Annabel. A golden rule. Never try. Just succeed. OK? Rule number one. In musicals and in life. Now scoot. Nine in the morning, on the dot, warmed up, ready to go. G'bye!

*(She exits as **LIZ** excitedly bursts in carrying piles of typed paper.)*

LIZ. What's the American for "Eureka"?

STACEY. Uh?

LIZ. New rewrite pages twenty-nine to thirty-eight, forty-four and forty-five, sixty-three to seventy-three.

(She plonks them on the table.)

As per instructions.

STACEY. We gave them twenty-nine to thirty-eight at lunchtime.

LIZ. Those were the ordinary rewrites. These are the re-rewrites. You said you wanted them by six.

STACEY. That's right. By six. Before I broke them for the day.

*(**LIZ** looks at her watch, realises she's too late.)*

LIZ. Ah. Sorry. It's just that sixty-three to seventy-three was a pig. It meant —

STACEY. It doesn't matter!

LIZ. Oh. I thought it did!

STACEY. No – for the staggeringly-simple reason that we'll be rewriting these again before the week's out.

LIZ. *(baffled)* They may be <u>alright</u>...

STACEY. Liz. In a musical <u>nothing's</u> alright until it's too late to be changed, *(a beat)* And when draft seven's printed, the same goes for that.

LIZ. The same what?

STACEY. It'll be rewritten. And then rewritten. And, after that, rewritten.

*(**LIZ** stares at him.)*

LIZ. Stacey. It's the final rehearsal script.

STACEY. *(amused)* Liz. That's what final rehearsal scripts, are <u>for</u>.

(Smiles at her)

Baby, you ain't even started. The rewriting doesn't stop till the night we open.

LIZ. In Manchester.

STACEY. The night we open in Manchester is when it starts for real. <u>Really</u> for real. When we open in the West End, then it stops. You'll know when: your hand drops off.

(She smiles. Shrugs.)

Liz, for a hit – it's worth it. <u>Anything's</u> worth it.

LIZ. I suppose so. Sorry.

(She goes over to the other table.)

I'll pour you a cup of tea? I'll use my other hand.

STACEY. No, thanks.

*(She pours tea for herself and takes it to the table. Sits down. **STACEY** smiles at her. Confident. Relaxed.)*

STACEY. Well, Author? Happy?

(She looks at him. A pause.)

LIZ. How do you mean?

STACEY. *(puzzled)* The rehearsals.

LIZ. Oh, the rehearsals. Very. May I make a suggestion?

STACEY. Make.

LIZ. Your coat's gorgeous. Can I touch it?

STACEY. Is that your suggestion?

LIZ. Umm... No.

STACEY. Gonna have fun, yeah?

LIZ. What?

STACEY. The rehearsals.

LIZ. Oh, yeah!

STACEY. So far so good, yeah?

LIZ. So far <u>very</u> good.

STACEY. Well now I'll tell you a little secret. Usually reserved for nervous investors in Fort Knox. For this stage of rehearsal, I've never known a show be in better shape.

LIZ. Really?

STACEY. Never. So – any complaints?

LIZ. Well, just one. You <u>know</u> the one.

STACEY. Liz. <u>Trust</u> me. Annabel's going to be sensational. When she's up there, opening night, with a full orchestra –

LIZ. Stacey, she can't act. At all. It's like asking my Auntie Bella to play Richard the Third. *(beat)* As a matter of fact, my Auntie Bella's available.

STACEY. Annabel's good. For fourth lead she's more than good.

LIZ. Stacey, I think she's wrong.

STACEY. She's gold.

LIZ. She was wrong when she auditioned, and she's even more wrong now.

STACEY. *(stiffly)* That ship has sailed, Liz! Forget it!

(**LIZ** *is a little thrown by his dismissiveness.*)

(*A silence.*)

STACEY. How about what I'm doing with the street scene? With the car-horns integrated into the music?

LIZ. I think it's brilliant. It's terrific. I've never seen anything <u>like</u> that before.

STACEY. Know why, young lady? 'Cause it ain't never been <u>done</u> before!

(He smiles. Pats her hand, reassuringly.)

So, just trust me, OK?

LIZ. *(smiles)* OK.

*(**BEBE** wanders in, wearing hat and coat)*

BEBE. Hi there.

STACEY. How'd your afternoon go?

BEBE. What can I tell you? I'm bushed. Three radio interviews, two TV, I'd lose less adrenalin writing a goddamn symphony. For a six-hundred-piece orchestra. A six-hundred-piece orchestra of tone-deaf-baboons. Tone-deaf <u>English</u> baboons. Ask me if I was wonderful.

LIZ. Were you wonderful?

BEBE. I got by. I got by. They loved me. *(to **STACEY**)* How'd <u>your</u> afternoon go?

STACEY. What can I tell you?

LIZ. It went terrific. He means terrific.

BEBE. No problems?

(A tiny beat.)

STACEY. Um... The duet *Long Time No See* ...

BEBE. Works like a dream, right? Best thing I ever wrote. <u>I</u> didn't even write it. My heart wrote it. The beats are heart-beats. Beautiful song.

STACEY. From the second chorus, I'm playing it Dixieland.

*(A stunned silence. **BEBE** turns slowly to face him. He stares.)*

LIZ. *(apprehensively)* Would you like a cup of tea, Bebe?

BEBE. *(statement)* Dixieland.

STACEY. Dixieland.

BEBE. *(erupting)* It's a goddamn <u>waltz</u>, you bum!! You want Dixieland, I'll write you Dixieland! What you <u>do not</u> do with a waltz of mine is profane the goddamn sonofabitch! OK, you got some bright idea — with your swanky collar turned up — fine, I'll throw the waltz away! Twenty-eight Broadway shows I thought I'd seen it all!

STACEY. Liz. "Long Time No See". This afternoon. Did it or did it not work in Dixie tempo?

BEBE. You ask her? Her first musical and she's Chief Attorney to the Supreme Court. Forget it. I'll write a new tune.

STACEY. Bebe! You-don't-have-to-write-a-new-tune!!

BEBE. Whatever I want to throw out I throw out. It's in my contract. I can write Handel's *Messiah* and throw it out. *Long Time No See* goes. I'll save it for my <u>next</u> musical. And in my next musical, it'll stop the show. Tomorrow morning, a.m., you get a new number, so help me God.

(A pause)

LIZ. Did I <u>ask</u> if you wanted tea, Bebe?

BEBE. Ah, to hell with it, why play games? Tomorrow morning, a.m., you get a new <u>composer</u>. I'm off the show as of now. I'm calling Theo's office, get a reservation. I go back Concorde.

STACEY. So go!

BEBE. I'm going!

(BEBE crosses to the telephone.)

LIZ. Bebe, when Stacey tried it as Dixieland – it was only from the second release —

BEBE. Comden and Greene, nineteen sixty-two, Arlington Theatre, Act Two Scene Three — they did a <u>Dixieland</u> in <u>waltz</u> tempo!

STACEY. *(correcting him)* Act <u>One</u> Scene Three.

BEBE. Act One, Act Two, same bucket of shit. The show closed after <u>six days</u>!

STACEY. They had money problems.

BEBE. Goddamn <u>Dixie</u> problems!!

(A silence. LIZ makes a move to start gathering her things together.)

LIZ. See you tomorrow, men.

STACEY. Stay where you are.

LIZ. Oh. Right.

(She sits down again.)

BEBE. Jerry Robbins once threw <u>out</u> a Dixieland finale to a waltz – Forty Second Street Theatre, nineteen seventy-two – the night before the <u>opening</u> night...!

STACEY. You want Jerry Robbins to direct the show?

BEBE. No one <u>mentioned</u> Jerry Robbins.

STACEY. You want Jerry Robbins to direct the show? Hal Prince? Martin Charnin? Fine. OK. Go ahead. I go home. Not tomorrow. <u>Tonight</u>. I'll be in New York <u>before</u> Concorde! *(to LIZ, who vainly attempts to answer)* Well? You're the author. Say the word. You want Jerry Robbins? One of the best? You'd like a more conventional approach to your book? Say so now. I'll go back to civilisation. Ah, what the hell. I'm off the show as of now!

(He crosses to the piano)

BEBE. I just beat you to it, pal!

(He crosses to the telephone.)

*(**LIZ** looks helplessly from one to the other.)*

LIZ. I mean...I mean you're both grown men... Can't you let bygones be... Um...can't you just forgive and for — I can't believe what's coming out of my mouth...

BEBE. *(to LIZ)* OK. "You're the author", he says. Big deal. Speaking as the author, who's right, him or me?

*(**LIZ** looks from one to the other.)*

LIZ. I've never done a musical before...

BEBE. You bet your sweet bippy! Go Dixieland in a waltz, you'll never do <u>another</u>!

STACEY. *(to* **LIZ***)* Well? Him or me?

LIZ. Oh, Christ...

STACEY. It's simple. Which one of us do you want?

*(***LIZ*** looks from one to the other. She starts laughing.)*

BEBE. You thought of a good gag? Great. Stick it in Act Two – it needs it!

*(***MIKE*** enters, carrying pages of lyric rewrites and briefcase.)*

MIKE. Stacey. Rewrite lyrics for *Whatever Happened to Tomorrow?* Three different versions, as requested, according to whether you decide on it solo or to chorus reprise it in Scene Nine.

(He glances away fractionally)

Bebe, Liz.

(He turns back to **STACEY***)*

I suppose, at a pinch, we can leave one verse open, in case we find a way of...

(He looks back at everyone's faces)

What's wrong?

(A short silence)

BEBE. Anyhow, Jerry Robbins isn't available. He's setting up a musical of Watergate in Boston.

MIKE. What?

LIZ. So, are you going?

BEBE. I'm calling a cab. If anyone ever goddamn well answers.

MIKE. What's wrong?

*(***LIZ*** laughs)*

MIKE. So, I go home to re-do this lyric – you're not going to believe this – and seven Lithuanian nymphomaniacs are lying on the kitchen floor. Stark naked. I was disgusted. I mean, I've never had it with seven Lithuanian nymphomaniacs before. Well, never if you don't count New Year's Eve. And certainly not on quarry tiles. The things they did to me with our Kenwood Blender. And I mean, it's not even under guarantee. I'll be useless tonight. There I was, just starting on the fourth nymphomaniac when Valerie walks in from Sainsbury's. So, "What are you doing with these seven Lithuanian nymphomaniacs?" she says. So I told her they were from the Gas Board. She's not a bad kid. She just said, "Thank God they've finally sent <u>someone</u>." *(a beat)* What's wrong?

STACEY. Let's see the new lyric.

LIZ. So are you staying?

(**MIKE** *hands him the lyric rewrites*)

MIKE. I think I've done what you wanted. Trouble is, I'm not all that sure it's as good as the original.

STACEY. *(with the most fractional of glances through the pages)* It's terrific. It's all terrific. Lose that one. I told you about that one. Trust me. *(to LIZ)* OK. Yours.

LIZ. My what?

STACEY. Rewrites.

LIZ. Er...what about them?

STACEY. Let's see them! I'm not telepathic, Liz! I can't read a script without <u>reading</u> it, OK? For Hal Prince it may be different, I can't speak for Hal Prince.

(**LIZ** *hands him her rewrites*)

LIZ. I've managed all the changes you asked for. I just hope the original wasn't better...I mean, here and there, I'm sure we —

STACEY. *(flicking through pages)* Terrific.

LIZ. *(pointing to the page)* I'm a bit worried about this bit...

STACEY. This bit's terrific. It's all terrific.

(*He reads on a few lines.*)

Lose that speech. Put that line there. Swap these with those. Cut that.

LIZ. *(face falling)* <u>Cut</u> it?

*(***STACEY*** hacks through the line with a thick red pencil)*

STACEY. Like it's never been.

LIZ. Stacey, it's a good line...

STACEY. That ship has sailed, Liz. So's the line.

BEBE. You're going to stand there and let him do that?

LIZ. What?

BEBE. You're the <u>author</u> for Chrissake! They're your words! Words are precious jewels – precious – tell him to piss off.

MIKE. What's wrong?

*(***BEBE*** starts to exit)*

BEBE. I'll give your regards to Broadway.

STACEY. G'bye!

BEBE. You said it, pal!

MIKE. *(to* **LIZ***)* Is something wrong?

(As **BEBE** *is doing up his coat,* **THEO** *bustles in)*

THEO. So how's absolutely the best creative team in the goddamn world? Fruitful day? *(to* **BEBE***)* You're not staying, Bebe-baby?

BEBE. Ask the smart-ass with the collar turned up. Like, hallelujah, all of a sudden a turned-up collar means you're Cecil B. de Mille. Been great working with you pal!

(He storms out. **THEO** *watches him go, puzzled, then turns to the others.)*

THEO. I think maybe I missed the gist, What's with Bebe?

STACEY. Sit down. We got a problem.

THEO. Problem?

STACEY. OK. The problem is as follows. There's a hallowed tradition in the making of musicals. Upheld by the likes of our dear Bebe Kaiser. Well, come to think of it, there <u>are</u> no likes of Bebe Kaiser – there's just Bebe Kaiser. The tradition is that a musical grows like a rose-bush. You water it in blood, sweat and tears. And the minute it buds – you smother it in manure.

THEO. You had a slight gentleman's disagreement, you two. I got the vibes. A producer has a sixth sense about these things...

STACEY. He's getting nervous because it's going so easy. The show's looking great, so he thinks it must be shit. There's no bleeding, no sweating, no tears. And it's breaking his heart. Now, you're the producer —

THEO. That <u>is</u> my function. Legally and morally. And the producer, in the final analysis —

STACEY. The producer, in the final analysis, gets off his ass, kicks Bebe in his and tells him times have changed since Madam Butterfly – and that we got work to do. Whatever work I <u>say</u>. Me. As per contract. <u>Everybody's</u> contract.

LIZ. Incidentally, Theo, talking about contracts —

THEO. *(to* **STACEY***)* I'll tell him, I'll tell him. As the producer, I'll —

LIZ. I mean, it's nine months now, Theo. And I've still had nothing to sign —

THEO. I'll approach the matter firmly but politely, as a gentleman —

LIZ. I was supposed to get a thousand pounds advance.

THEO. I'll say, "Bebe," I'll say —

LIZ. I've had nothing and my agent —

THEO. Liz, for Chrissake, will you stop trouble-making!! You're a trouble-maker! You make trouble! Just don't keep throwing your weight around all the time! Just write me a beautiful book — *(to* **MIKE***)* and <u>you</u> stick to writing "moon" and "June" and leave me to worry about contracts, OK!

LIZ. That's all I was asking —

MIKE. I didn't even ask <u>anything</u>...!

THEO. *(to* LIZ*)* Just don't be such a big-mouth. It ain't ladylike!

STACEY. Theo?

THEO. Yes, my friend.

STACEY. You ever see me lose my temper?

THEO. I...er...I don't think so...

STACEY. You'd know. You'd know. I turn into the Incredible Hulk. It's incredible.

THEO. Uh?

STACEY. I told you what to do about Bebe. I spelled it out. Now do it! Move! Go!

(THEO, *scared, starts immediately to exit as* BEBE *strolls back in.)*

BEBE. Hi, Theo. Liz, do I get a copy of them rewrites or do I call the Operator and ask to be put through to Information?

LIZ. Are you staying then?

THEO. <u>Again</u> with her big mouth! Bebe...um...there's something Stacey wishes me to discuss with you... Stacey happened to mention, as he has a <u>right</u> to do, as we all have a <u>right</u> to do...nothing to worry about... in the course of normal conversation...

BEBE. Stacey's a pain in the ass.

(STACEY, *ominously calm, looks at* THEO*)*

STACEY. Theo?

THEO. Now, Bebe-baby...

BEBE. You're a pain in the ass, Golden Boy.

STACEY. Up yours, Kaiser.

BEBE. The principal reason you're a pain in the ass – *(to* THEO*)* You'll excuse the language – *(to* STACEY*)* is that you're <u>right</u> about the Dixieland.

LIZ. <u>What</u>???

THEO. Dixieland?

MIKE. Dixieland??

LIZ. I don't believe it!

BEBE. He's right. Why – you want to argue? With your vast experience of the musical theatre, you want to fight? You're gonna tell me what's possible in a musical and what ain't? Well, let me tell you, Miss Know-It-All! Anything's possible!

STACEY. Good! I'm going over to Lawrence's place to see the set designs.

LIZ. Um...Stacey, could we go for a quiet drink somewhere and work on the re-re-rewrites? Jim's not expecting me back till later.

STACEY. Sorry, Liz. No can do. No can do. 'Night gang.

(STACEY exits)

THEO. OK everybody? Fruitful day, thank you. *(to STACEY's back)* Stacey, I'll share the cab.

(THEO exits)

BEBE. Hang in there, Theo. I'll share the cab as well.

(BEBE moves towards exit, then stops and turns to MIKE)

BEBE. Mike, a bone to pick with you. I have a little difference of opinion with Stacey – with anyone – I expect loyalty from you. You're my ally. Composer and lyricist are collaborators. We stick together right or wrong. Right or wrong! The observance of which concept is what made America great and the ignoring of which made England England. OK? In our entire discussion I did not hear one goddamn squeak out of you!

(MIKE boggles at him.)

MIKE. I – wasn't – here! I didn't know what it was about! It was before I walked in! I kept asking "What's wrong?...

BEBE. Collaborators, OK? Same side. Comrades and buddies, got it?

MIKE. Yeah.

BEBE. You taking me to dinner tonight? Chinese.

MIKE. Um...well...as a matter of fact. Val's expecting me to bring —

BEBE. So bring her along! I'll wear a buttonhole! Pick me up at the Hilton, nine, nine-thirty.

*(**BEBE** exits. A silence.)*

MIKE. Which brings us to the burning question: Have you ever had it manacled hand and foot to the Eddistone Lighthouse with sixteen Albino slaves, bearing Tupperware dildoes, and pandering to your every sensual whim?

LIZ. Twice. It's not all it's cracked up to be.

MIKE. Val's mother said the same. Her very words. And after all that he <u>still</u> went without the rewrites.

LIZ. Who?

MIKE. Bebe.

LIZ. Oh, Bebe!

(A silence)

MIKE. Home-time.

*(He picks up his rewrites and takes them to **LIZ**)*

I'll take your new stuff.

(They exchange rewrites)

There's mine. *(a beat)* Not that they're new any more.

(A pause. They hand each other's rewrites back.)

LIZ. How's Valerie these days?

MIKE. Better than nothing! Alright, I think. I never have time to ask her. All <u>she</u> ever says is "How's it gone today?" and I say "Terrific". And then I say "Have the kids been good?" and she says "Is that a new lyric?"

LIZ. I know. It's the same with me and Jim. All he ever says is "If you get a million pounds shall we get a house in Hampstead or Knightsbridge?" And I say "It may only be half a million – it may have to be a flat".

*(**LIZ** sits on piano keys. **MIKE** is seated at piano.)*

He's gone impotent.

MIKE. Me too! Sometimes in bed I say, "Val, I'm still impotent" and she says, "Is that a new lyric?" and I say "Yes" and we go to sleep. Do you and Jim laugh about it?

LIZ. Not laugh exactly. Jim <u>cries</u>. And then I pull his pyjamas down and sing two choruses of *Long Time No See* – in Dixieland —

*(***MIKE*** echoes)*

– and then we nod off. Exciting though, isn't it?

MIKE. Not at all.

LIZ. The show.

MIKE. Oh, the <u>show</u>. Terrific.

LIZ. It's the most exciting time I've ever known. He's the most incredible director. I think he's a genius. Superman.

MIKE. I think he is. I keep wondering if he can walk on water. *(a beat)* I also wonder if it's going to be any good.

LIZ. What?

MIKE. The show.

LIZ. How do you mean?

MIKE. I sometimes get a sort of niggling feeling. Impotence apart. Still...if <u>Stacey</u> says so...

LIZ. Exactly!

MIKE. Yeah. You're right. You ain't seen nothing yet, kid. Just wait till you hear a twenty-piece orchestra instead of just this...

He nods towards piano

And when they're all on the actual stage *(plays chord)* With lighting *(plays chord)* And sets *(plays chord)* And costumes *(plays chord)* It's magic *(plays chord) (a beat)* Of course, <u>you</u> know and <u>I</u> know it's sleight-of-hand. <u>And</u> Val. But it <u>looks</u> like magic. *(beat)* Come to dinner with us?

LIZ. And Bebe? With his buttonhole! No thanks.

MIKE. *(takes the point, laughs)* Sorry.

LIZ. Sad, isn't he?

MIKE. Who?

LIZ. Bebe. And Stacey.

MIKE. Sad? They've never been happier! They love every second of it.

LIZ. I know. That's the bit that's <u>sad</u>. <u>Why</u> they're sad... They don't even <u>know</u> they are...

MIKE. *(baffled)* I think I'll stick to writing "moon" and "June".

LIZ. Forget it. Hey, I meant to ask you. Have you ever had cunnilingus with a killer-whale?

MIKE. Christ, Liz! You've broken my dream!

(**LIZ** *laughs at being topped.* **MIKE** *grins.*)

See you tomorrow, pal.

LIZ. See you.

(**MIKE** *exits.*)

(*Offstage, he sees* **THEO**)

MIKE. *(offstage)* Theo! What are you doing, lurking in the dark?

THEO. *(offstage)* Who's lurking? I'm allowed to lurk.

(**THEO** *enters. Watches* **LIZ** *getting her things together*)

Listen. I was thinking. No reason. Silly sitting around your place on your own...you could come round to my hotel later. No ulterior motive. Speaking as a gentleman. I could...um...fry you some eggs.

(**LIZ** *smiles, shakes her head.*)

LIZ. See you tomorrow, Theo.

(**LIZ** *exits.*)

THEO. "Whatever Happened to Tomorrow?"

(*He looks at mess on table and starts collecting dirty mugs together.*)

(*The phone rings.* **THEO** *crosses and picks up the receiver.*)

(into phone) Mulberry Street Rehearsal Rooms – you're too late, everyone's gone home.

(Pause)

Debra! What the hell are you doing in the office after six o'clock, apart from screwing me for overtime? What's the problem?

(Pause)

OK, Debra, OK. I'll call him in the morning. I'll tell him, firmly but politely, we haven't had his investment yet, the schmock, and would he please let us have his cheque for forty-thousand pounds at once, he's investing in a hit show, could we please see the colour of his money, thank you, *kush mir in tuchass.* Alright?

(Pause)

THEO. *(into phone)* Debra, I'm very grateful for your concern. It's very touching in one so young. Please, Debra, have a little respect for my grey hairs. And my judgement.

(Pause)

Debra, would I jeopardise the biggest smash of all time by being under-capitalised?? Please, Debra. A little commonsense. If I was a peasant from Nebbish County, would I be a producer?

Scene Three

(A hotel room in Manchester, Spring.)

(It's the early hours of the morning. **LIZ**, *wearing pyjamas, is seated at the dressing table, typing rewrites.)*

(The bed, the dressing table, the floor, are all littered and strewn with sheets of typed paper, handwritten paper and screwed up balls of paper.)

(The radio is playing late-night, romantic pop-music.)

*(***LIZ*** is exhausted and dishevelled. Smoking constantly. Typing in frenzied bursts which are punctuated by blank "think" periods while she stares at her reflection in the dressing table mirror.)*

(The music on the radio fades out.)

D.J. *(on radio)* Dreamy...but nice. You're listening to "Dreamy But Nice" here on Radio North West keeping you warm and cosy, nice and dreamy in the wee small hours. Earlier tonight, I had as my special guest here in the studio – a very special guest indeed. He came hot-foot straight from our very own Palace Theatre the moment the curtain came down on the Manchester premiere of his new musical *Whatever Happened to Tomorrow?*

(During this, **LIZ** *stops typing and turns the radio a little louder. She sorts out the papers on the bed whilst listening.)*

He's the composer of over twenty Broadway musicals, a legend-in-his-own-lifetime, Mr. Bebe Kaiser. I talked to him.

LIZ. But did he <u>listen</u>? Did he <u>listen</u>?

D.J. *(on radio)* Mr. Kaiser. Welcome to Manchester.

BEBE. *(on radio)* It's my very great pleasure and privilege to be here. Incidentally, the...um...the "over twenty"

Broadway musicals you so kindly referred to...the actual number's twenty-eight.

D.J. *(on radio)* Oh, twenty-eight, right.

BEBE. *(on radio)* I've worked with the great and the near-great from Eddie Cantor to Liza Minelli, God bless her, I love her.

D.J. *(on radio)* Right on. Now, tell me, Mr. Kaiser, how did the show go?

BEBE. *(on radio)* What can I tell you – we got a hit. The audience fell in love with it.

D.J. *(on radio)* And now it's next stop London, right?

BEBE. *(on radio)* Correct. We got four more weeks here on the road to get the show right, then we go —

D.J. *(on radio)* To get it right?

BEBE. *(on radio)* Excuse me?

LIZ. Ah!

D.J. *(on radio)* You've still to get it right?

BEBE. *(on radio)* This is an out-of-town run. That's what we're here for. This is where the work gets done. A little polishing, maybe a new scene or two, maybe a new song or two —

LIZ. Slash a wrist or two.

D.J. *(on radio)* But, as it stands now, the show isn't really right?

LIZ. Wriggle out of that one Bebe-baby!

BEBE. *(on radio)* Only in the sense of not quite perfect. For the West End it'll be <u>more</u> than perfect.

LIZ. Well wriggled Bebe-baby.

D.J. *(on radio)* Mr. Kaiser, I'd like to talk to you a little more about your early days before you became successful —

BEBE. *(on radio)* Well, <u>that</u> won't take too long!

D.J. *(on radio)* No. Right. And we'll have that little talk right after this next record.

BEBE. *(on radio)* One of mine, I hope.

D.J. *(on radio)* Of course.

BEBE. *(on radio)* That'll be my very great pleasure and privilege.

LIZ. And this will be mine. *(Switches radio off)*

(She then picks up the telephone receiver.)

(into phone) Room service? Miss Morris here, Room Three-three-nine. Can I have a pot of coffee and a chicken sandwich, please? *(beat)* Yes, chicken.

(There's a knock at the door (Offstage R))

Absolutely the fastest chicken in the world. Come in.

*(**THEO** enters. He looks weary and wan.)*

Ah!

THEO. Hi! Stacey said you'd be working. If it's not convenient – a professional call – just say. I'll go to bed and dream about money.

LIZ. No, no, you're fine, come in. Do you want anything? I've just rung room service.

THEO. Thank you, no. I've been drinking champagne since the curtain came down. More than's good for me. Even more than's <u>bad</u> for me. May I sit down? I need to sit down.

*(He sits in the armchair on two piles of rewrites. **LIZ** vainly attempts to grab them before he sits on them.)*

Thank you. Why do I even ask? I'm paying for the goddamn room in the first place. Your room, Mike's room, Stacey's suite, Bebe's <u>double</u>-suite. I'm allowed to use one lousy chair.

LIZ. Well, Theo? It's finally on the stage. Excited?

THEO. I just spent an hour with Stacey. I never seen anyone so excited. Even for an American. Maybe with the possible exception of Kermit the whatisit –

LIZ. Frog.

THEO. Frog. He can talk, that Stacey. It's only after I've left him that I...

(He peters away into a sigh)

He's convinced London will be a million times better than tonight. A million times a bigger smash.

LIZ. He gave me a million rewrites to do. For tomorrow.

(She resumes typing. A pause.)

THEO. *(tearful)* Liz, I'll tell you how I'm feeling. To tell you the truth, I'm a little depressed. A little low.

(He sighs.)

He wants to change the sets. Throw them away. Never see them again. Eighty thousand pounds' worth. He hates them.

LIZ. He always <u>loved</u> them! He said they were terrific.

THEO. Love and hate – it's a very thin dividing line. I been married four times. I know about these things. *(beat)* He also wants to throw out six of Bebe's numbers. <u>Six</u>. Bebe don't know yet.

(He sighs)

Which is why I'm alive to tell the tale. He also wants to change the lighting, three of the orchestral arrangements, most of the lyrics —

LIZ. And three scenes in Act One and two in Act Two... You're sitting on half of them.

(The phone rings.)

THEO. Maybe that's him?

LIZ. It'll be the first time if it is.

THEO. I mean, don't he call about the rewrites?

LIZ. Oh. Yes. He calls about the rewrites.

(She takes the phone)

(into phone) Hello? *(a beat: she sighs)* Yes, Bebe. Yes I did. Yes, <u>all</u> of it. It was impossible to switch off.

THEO. The broadcast.

LIZ. *(into phone)* Yes, Bebe, you were absolutely fascinating. *(pause)* Yes, absolutely terrific, *(pause)* Pardon? *(pause)* Um... No, Bebe. It's very nice of you but it's very late and I'm working. *(pause)* Yes, Bebe, I <u>know</u> I do. We <u>all</u>

look as though we need a little fun. Thanks anyway. *(pause)* Bebe, I'm very grateful for the offer, but I'm not in the <u>least</u> bit lonely, Theo's here.

THEO. *(guiltily)* "In his professional capacity" tell him.

LIZ. *(into phone)* In his professional capacity, with his trousers on. *(a beat)* Yes. Hang on. *(to* **THEO***)* He'd like a word in your ear. He didn't specify which.

*(***THEO*** takes the phone.)*

THEO. *(into phone)* So what can I do for my favourite composer – I've worked with them all – Did I ever tell you a lie? *(pause)* What? *(pause)* That's all? OK. Goodnight.

(He replaces the receiver.)

(to **LIZ***)* He says to tell you you're a stuck-up, tight assed, frigid, English bitch.

LIZ. Oh, that's nice. In one of his <u>better</u> moods was he?

*(***THEO*** sighs)*

THEO. Before meeting with Stacey, I had five minutes with the cast. *(pause)* They were all crying. Everywhere I looked — grown men, women, sobbing their hearts out. I thought, maybe it's the excitement of opening night. But no-one stopped crying long enough to tell me.

LIZ. They're always crying. They've been crying for weeks. All day in rehearsals. Afterwards in the Wimpey Bar. The poor sods are exhausted. All the screaming. All the changes...

THEO. "All the screaming, all the changes" she says! It's all the <u>crying</u>! <u>Crying</u> makes us exhausted.

(A pause)

LIZ. Sometimes <u>I</u> try to cry. I sit in front of this mirror while I'm typing. And I look at myself. And I try to cry.

(She jerks her head back and forth like a pecking hen.)

The tears won't come, though. So then I ring Jim to feel better and want to cry even more. One night I rang him and <u>he</u> was crying, He was peeling onions. These normal human beings – they get everywhere...

(She looks at **THEO***)*

I should be cooking his dinner, not <u>him</u>. What the hell am I doing here, Theo?

*(***THEO*** is sitting staring into space.)*

THEO. Mike wasn't crying. But he wasn't happy. *(a beat)* He thinks we got us a bum director.

(He looks at her questioningly for her reaction. She avoids his look.)

LIZ. And Bebe?

*(***THEO*** sighs. Stares into space again.)*

THEO. Bebe <u>knows</u> we got us a bum director. He also thinks your book should be recycled. Preferably into Kleenex. *(a beat)* Then I met with Stacey. And he said, "Do you mind if I intellectualise?" and I said "Be my guest," and he said, "The score is shit, the lyrics are shit and the book is shit". And then he said —

LIZ. "Trust me."

THEO. He's <u>very</u> happy, bless him.

(A worried pause.)

LIZ. And you?

THEO. Me?

(He turns to her – almost angrily.)

Listen, it's a <u>musical</u>! <u>Every</u> musical has times like these. <u>All</u> the time they have times like these, *(a beat)* I'm very happy. <u>Very</u>. *(a beat)* He also wants to change half the choreography and most of the costumes. *(a pause)* And you? What do <u>you</u> think?

*(***LIZ*** wrestles worriedly with her feelings.)*

LIZ. *(slowly, tentatively feeling her way)* I think that we're probably in trouble. *(a pause)* I also think that Stacey'll get us out.

THEO. It's Stacey that got us i<u>n</u>!

LIZ. I know. I think he'll, most probably, get us out.

(There's a knock at the door. (Offstage R))

I hope it's not the thirteen New Zealand Rugby forwards. I'm not in the mood. Come in.

*(A **WAITRESS** enters R, carrying a tray of coffee and sandwiches.)*

WAITRESS. Room service.

*(The **WAITRESS** stands looking for somewhere to put the tray. Every surface is covered with pages of script.)*

WAITRESS. Coffee and cheese sandwiches it is.

LIZ. Cheese? Didn't I ask for chicken?

WAITRESS. We had no chicken, Miss, as luck would have it. So I brought, well, the nearest to it, like, you know, the next best thing. Cheese.

*(**LIZ** sighs. Looks round for a space.)*

LIZ. Right, can you find a...um. There must be...

(She finally moves pages of script from the luggage rack.)

WAITRESS. Ta.

(She puts the tray down.)

If you'd just sign, Miss.

LIZ. Oh, yes.

*(She signs the bill and hands it back to the **WAITRESS**.)*

Hang on, don't go. Where's my handbag?

THEO. You want ten p?

LIZ. Well, twenty p might be nicer.

THEO. *(feels in his pocket for change)* Since I pay for everything anyway... Nah! Fifteen.

(**THEO** *gives the money to the* **WAITRESS**. *The* **WAITRESS** *is standing looking round at the mess the room is in.*)

WAITRESS. Didn't the chambermaid do your room for you? That's Marjorie to a T that is. It's her floor. She's a right lazy cow.

(*She bends down and starts picking up piles of paper.*)

Mind you, she hasn't had an easy life...

LIZ. (*suddenly noticing*) Ah – no. I didn't <u>want</u> her to do it...to disturb anything...it's deliberate...well, not <u>deliberate</u> exactly...I'm working.

WAITRESS. I know.

LIZ. Mmm?

WAITRESS. The Hall Porter told me it's you that's putting on the concert at the Palace.

(**LIZ** *throws her a puzzled glance. Then shares a smile with* **THEO**.)

LIZ. The...um...<u>musical</u>, yes.

WAITRESS. Yes, that's right. He was <u>saying</u>. And are you in charge of it then?

LIZ. In charge of it? No, I'm just...actually, this gentleman's in charge of it, really.

(**THEO** *grimaces at* **LIZ**. *Shakes his head at her not to involve him.*)

WAITRESS. (*looking at* **THEO**) Oh, I see. Very nice. It'll be a good job, that. (*a beat*) I went tonight.

THEO. (*not interested, impatient*) What?

WAITRESS. Before I came on. I'm on twelve till eight. I prefer nights. So I went before I came on.

THEO. Went? Went where?

WAITRESS. To your concert – doodah – musical. (*a beat*) It wasn't bad.

THEO. (*dismissively*) Thank you.

LIZ. Thank you.

WAITRESS. A bit, you know, slow in parts, a bit boring. The
    <u>scenery</u> was nice, though. I liked the scenery.

*(WAITRESS makes for exit. THEO watches her go and
then he and LIZ exchange a glance.)*

LIZ. Excuse me! Was there...was there anything else you
    liked?

*(The WAITRESS turns and comes back into the room. She
ponders. LIZ and THEO wait. THEO indicates to LIZ
that he thinks she's crazy.)*

WAITRESS. Um... Not really. Well, the <u>dresses</u> I suppose.
    Some of them. I mean, it's very hard to say what you
    like, isn't it, when something's not true to life.

LIZ. Uh?

WAITRESS. You know, when something's so far-fetched.

LIZ. Far-fetched?

WAITRESS. Well, they're never really true to life, are they,
    things like that? I mean, if someone's like <u>heart</u>-broken
    say, and, you know, breaking their hearts – well, they
    don't start <u>singing</u> do they? They just sort of, well,
    break their hearts, really.

(A pause)

LIZ. Well...that's what happens in musicals. People sing.

WAITRESS. Yes. That's what I'm saying. They do. It's not
    true to life. I mean, take whatsername – the main part
    – the GI bride — Helen Something – Helen...

LIZ. Helen Grace? That's the name of the actress – not the
    character.

WAITRESS. Yes, well, her. I mean, she came out with some
    right tripe, didn't she?

(A bristly pause.)

LIZ. Well, she has to say more or less what's written for her,
    really.

*(**THEO**, a little less patiently than before, signals **LIZ** to
get rid of her.)*

WAITRESS. *(doubtful)* Mmm. I'm not saying she doesn't take a good part, she <u>does</u>. That's half the trouble, really, isn't it?

LIZ. What is?

WAITRESS. Well, tonight you see her pretending to be a GI bride or whatever.

LIZ. A GI bride. Yes.

WAITRESS. And then another time, say on the telly, you see her pretending to be a nun or a duchess or a heroine or something. In one advert she's cracked up to be an ordinary housewife doing the ironing. Well, if <u>that</u> isn't far-fetched, what is?

LIZ. It's...it's <u>acting</u>!

THEO. Liz! For Chrissake!

WAITRESS. Well, put like that, yes. If you look at it that way. Tonight, though, what was she pretending to be – GI bride apart?

LIZ. Not <u>pretending</u>! <u>Acting</u>!

WAITRESS. Acting, then. I mean, she was supposed to hate the feller, wasn't she, the husband?

LIZ. She pitied him.

*(A pause. The **WAITRESS** ponders. Then quietly, flatly, unemotionally —)*

WAITRESS. I hate <u>mine</u>. That's why I ask to come on nights. I've hated him for sixteen years. And he doesn't even know. Mind you, <u>I</u> don't <u>sing</u> about it. I <u>pretend</u>, though. Every day and every night for sixteen years. And he doesn't even know. *(a beat)* I'm a bit of an actress myself, really, in a way. You can clap if you like.

(She starts to exit.)

I'll come back after for the pots.

(She exits.)

THEO. Satisfied? You want waitresses' opinions? For months you work your balls off, young lady – you ask the janitor what he thinks of the characterisation? Serves you

right. She liked the scenery. Eighty-thousand pounds
in the garbage disposer.

(A silence. **LIZ** *sits motionless, troubled, deep in thought.)*

LIZ. *(quietly, sadly)* Oh, hell.

THEO. Oh, hell, what?

LIZ. I wonder if that's it.

THEO. Uh?

LIZ. I wonder.

THEO. If what's what?

LIZ. At least she knows it's only pretend. They don't. Their
whole bloody lives are pretend. They don't know the
difference. People only do that when they're sad.

THEO. Who? Who's sad? Waitresses?

LIZ. Bebe. And Stacey. *(a beat)* Not you, Theo – because
you're only doing it for the money. But those two.

THEO. Liz, I'm not Harold Pinter – unless you speak to me
in words I don't know what you're saying!

*(***LIZ*** *turns to him urgently.)*

LIZ. Theo. Listen. All this. It's only a <u>show</u>. A concert. It
doesn't <u>matter</u>.

THEO. Eh??

LIZ. The entire thing. The last few months – the next few.
None of it matters bloody <u>tuppence</u>!

THEO. The show?? Seven hundred thousand pounds don't
mean tuppence?? Look, Liz, this is middle-of-the-night
talk. Have some English Cheddar from New Zealand.

*(***LIZ*** *lets pages of rewrites she is holding fall to the floor.)*

LIZ. All these. Nothing. Not important.

(She turns to **THEO**.*)*

Think. Of all the things in life, is there <u>anything</u> –
anything at <u>all</u> – that matters less than a musical? Poor
Stacey.

*(She starts to laugh – then immediately puts her hand
over her mouth.)*

There's <u>nothing</u>, Theo. Nothing less important.

(A pause. She sighs.)

I feel so bloody tired...

THEO. We <u>all</u> feel tired.

(A pause)

LIZ. I've written ten million words and they're not true to life... <u>Now</u> I think I can cry.

THEO. *(yelling)* She's a <u>waitress</u>! A <u>dumb</u> waitress! Suddenly she's a theatre critic. She's Milton Whatshisname in drag? Listen, Wet Blanket, I'm sorry I'm only a producer not a waitress, but <u>I</u> tell you we got a <u>brilliant</u> show! The greatest. In the next four weeks, Stacey'll make it the greatest <u>ever</u>! We're going to —

(Suddenly we hear – very loudly – the clanking of a heavy automatic bell.)

*(**THEO** and **LIZ** look at each other.)*

THEO. Goddamn New York ambulances, in Manchester yet!

LIZ. *(scared)* It's the fire-bell. Jesus, two o'clock in the morning and someone sets the sodding hotel on fire. The show wasn't <u>that</u> bad...!

THEO. Tim Lloyd Webber and Andrew Rice. They stop at nothing.

*(**LIZ** races UR and tears down a card of fire instructions.)*

LIZ. *(reading)* "In case of fire, proceed quickly to fire-escape door at end of corridor. Do not use lift. Do not stop to collect valuables. Do not re-enter the building."

(She throws the card down on the dressing table.)

Come on, Theo! Move!

THEO. *(quietly)* Fire. *(suddenly realising)* FIRE! FIRE!

*(He races from the room, leaving **LIZ** looking for her handbag. After about 10 seconds, the **WAITRESS** bursts in.)*

WAITRESS. Miss! Fire alarm! Shift yourself!

LIZ. *(panicking)* I can't find my handbag!

WAITRESS. No valuables! Sod your sodding handbag!! Nothing! Your<u>self</u>!

*(She races out. **LIZ** races out after her. The alarm bell is still ringing. 20 seconds later **LIZ** rushes back in, scoops up armfuls of rewrites from the bed, the floor, the armchair, the floor. As she reaches the dressing-table, the alarm bell stops.)*

*(**LIZ**, her arms full of papers, wavers, undecided whether to stay or to leave.)*

*(**THEO** strolls nonchalantly back in.)*

THEO. Don't panic. A false alarm.

LIZ. What?

THEO. Bebe set off the fire alarm. He thought it might be good publicity.

*(**LIZ** drops her armful of rewrites to the floor, and slowly subsides on top of them. **THEO** calmly sits in the armchair and takes a cheese sandwich from the plate. With his other hand, he holds **LIZ**'s hand.)*

THEO. Listen. With the creative team we got, absolutely the best creative team in the world, we got...no, <u>nearly</u> got...on the <u>brink</u> of nearly got...the most stupendous, sure-fire, solid-gold hit in the history of the British theatre.

*(**THEO** lets **LIZ**'s hand drop.)*

Or. On the other hand. The most stupendous, sure-fire, whatisit flop.

LIZ. "Potential".

THEO. Potential. *(a beat)* So, I'm the producer. Tell me. Which is it to be? *(a beat)* Or not to be?

End of Act One

ACT TWO

(The stage of a West End theatre. A summer evening, about six o'clock.)

(The stage is in near-darkness. **STACEY** *enters from the wings, feeling his way uncertainly in the darkness.)*

(He shouts up at the **BOARD OPERATOR***)*

STACEY. OK! Let there be light!

(He continues walking. Nothing happens.)

I said "Let there be light"!

(He crashes into a chair. It hurts. He screams ferociously up at the **BOARD OPERATOR***.)*

For God's sake!

BOARD OP. *(offstage DR)* Hello. Board Operator speaking. You want the light on now, or what?

STACEY. If that's not too much trouble.

BOARD OP. *(offstage)* That's what I'm here for, innit mate!

(A spotlight is switched on – lighting just **STACEY***. He yells back at the* **BOARD OPERATOR***.)*

STACEY. Not just me, dummy! The stage! Light the goddamn stage! I appreciate this is England and you don't like moving your hand more than is absolutely necessary! I'd also appreciate it as one hell of a favour if you'd read your work-schedule now and then! It's now six o'clock. The producer called an official meeting. You're on duty till six-thirty, OK?

(All the lights are switched on at the same time.)

Terrific. Jesus. Thank you.

BOARD OP. *(offstage)* Don't you mention it, squire!

(The stage is bare apart from a skip, a couple of chairs and a few pieces of scenery upstage.)

*(**STACEY**'s carrying a clipboard. He wanders around the stage for a few moments, kicking his heels. He seems grim, agitated.)*

*(**THEO** comes rushing in. He seems nervous, defensive.)*

THEO. I'm sorry I'm late for the meeting. The others aren't here yet?

STACEY. *(biting his words, angrily)* There's a limit, Theo. I get driven <u>past</u> that limit, I hit out. OK? <u>Where</u> I hit is not my concern – I just hit. You ready for that?

(A pause)

THEO. You're annoyed, aren't you? That the others aren't here yet?

STACEY. Not them. They're in the Stage Manager's office, finalising the intro and out for *Long Time No See*. I'm not annoyed about them.

(A pause.)

THEO. *(puzzled)* Someone <u>else</u> maybe?

STACEY. *(wearily)* Was the Board Operator told I wanted the stage lit after six p.m.?

THEO. Sure. He misses half his supper break, he gets overtime. He's now on overtime.

STACEY. *(quietly, resignedly)* The stage wasn't lit. Every little damn thing I want doing, I have to give three pints of blood.

THEO. Stacey.

STACEY. Three pints a day. Sometimes <u>twice</u> a day. I'm running out of blood, Theo. *(a beat)* I'm OK for bile.

(A short pause.)

THEO. I'll talk to his superior, firmly but politely. He'll kick him in the ass.

(An uncomfortable silence.)

STACEY. So. Eleven days before a West End opening, a million and one things to do, you feel it incumbent to waste half an hour of my time with a meeting?

THEO. We need to talk.

*(A pause. **STACEY** looks at him, suspicious of **THEO**'s nervousness, evasiveness.)*

STACEY. About what, Theo?

THEO. We'll talk. We'll talk at the meeting.

STACEY. I understand, Theo. What is the mystery meeting <u>for</u>?

THEO. You say they're doing the intro and out for *Long Time No See*?

STACEY. That's right.

THEO. *(worried)* They did it in Manchester. The intro and out have <u>always</u> been there...

STACEY. Not the new ones.

THEO. Uh?

STACEY. *Long Time No See* is now going in Scene One.

THEO. What?

STACEY. As from tomorrow.

THEO. How?

STACEY. Beautifully, that's how. *(a beat)* It's now Latin American tempo.

*(**THEO** boggles at him.)*

I got this idea in the night.

THEO. *(incredulously)* At this <u>stage</u>...you want to switch <u>numbers</u>??

STACEY. It'll be terrific.

*(A pause. **THEO**'s now feeling almost sick.)*

THEO. Stacey. In all conscience. With the shape the show is in...

STACEY. It's in <u>great</u> shape.

THEO. Well, yes... In many ways in great shape... In many <u>more</u> ways...maybe <u>not</u> such great shape...

(**LIZ**, **BEBE** *and* **MIKE** *enter, carrying typewritten and handwritten sheets of paper.* **BEBE** *hands his papers to* **MIKE** *who crosses and hands them to* **STACEY**.)

THEO. *(to* **MIKE***) Long Time No See* now goes in Scene One, yes?

MIKE. Looks like it. Ask me again tomorrow.

(A pause.)

*(***STACEY** *looks round at each of them.)*

(They smile edgy, forced half-smiles back at him.)

THEO. I think we all sit down yes? Gentlemen – lady and gentlemen – maybe first on the agenda, we all sit down, right?

*(***THEO** *bustles offstage L, collects two chairs and places them in line with one of the others.* **BEBE**, **MIKE** *and* **LIZ** *sit.* **THEO** *sits DL then realises* **STACEY** *is still standing. He takes his chair across for him.)*

Oh, Stacey, I'm sorry.

*(***THEO** *then rushes UL and collects another chair which he places DL and sits.* **STACEY** *remains standing DR.)*

Everybody sitting down? Everybody...seated? Everybody comfortable...in a civilised manner? And so, therefore, if we open the meeting...and make a start...and so on and so forth...

STACEY. Theo. That's another ten seconds. In the ashcan. Lost forever. For Chrissake, get to the goddamn point!!

(A pause.)

*(***THEO** *nervously re-girds his loins.)*

THEO. For the past few weeks, Stacey, maybe you've noticed – you're an intelligent man and you've earned our <u>respect</u>...in that respect – maybe you've noticed that one or two of us have been a little concerned... maybe not <u>concerned</u> exactly...but, speaking as your producer —

STACEY. Speaking as your director, God help me, you've called a meeting to put me in the dock and bring me to trial. For the past few weeks, Mr. Producer-man, you've been giving me the <u>bad</u>-mouth... <u>Not</u> one or two of you – <u>all</u> of you... It started in rehearsal, it continued in Manchester – "Stacey's gone crazy. Stacey's killing the show".

(An uncomfortable silence.)

*(**MIKE** fidgets. **LIZ**, motionless, stares down at her shoes.)*

THEO. Stacey, no one would dream of saying that you were killing the...

BEBE. No one. That's an expression no one's...

STACEY. Listen...before the curtain goes up on any musical, there's a prologue – called the Witch's Ordeal. You spend a few months sticking dry twigs up the director's ass. Then, just before opening night, you set 'em on fire. If he burns he's guilty. If he's innocent he settles for a pretty sore ass. OK, light my fire, what's the charges? Shoot.

THEO. Stacey. Don't <u>upset</u> yourself! We're having a <u>discussion</u>...<u>discussing</u>... No one's on trial, for Chrissake! No one's killing <u>nothing</u>! *(a beat)* All I wanted to say, and I am sure the team will correct me if I'm wrong, is that there are maybe one or two small things...not <u>major</u> small things, <u>minor</u> small things... that we as —

STACEY. *(starting to go)* G'bye! I got the new designer to see. I'll be five minutes, tops.

*(He strides off into the wings. **THEO** shouts after him.)*

THEO. Stacey! I called an official Producer's Meeting.

STACEY. *(offstage)* I know. And when it <u>starts</u> I'll be there!

(A long pause.)

BEBE. Killing the show? He's hung, drawn and quartered it, buried it up to the neck in quicksand and kicked its goddamn face in. *(a beat)* And that's one hell of a way to go.

THEO. We'll tell him. When be gets back, we'll tell him all our complaints.

BEBE. All? I'll need thirty years minimum, weekends included. <u>Thanksgiving</u> included.

MIKE. I'll only need three seconds. "Stacey, we've had it: we'll close opening night."

*(**BEBE** begins to pace up and down.)*

BEBE. Let me tell you something – I been through this ball-game before. <u>I</u> know how to play it. <u>You</u> may need a little coaching. Right?

THEO. Right!

BEBE. Right, *(pause: gathers his thoughts)* When the smart-ass with the reversible sleeve-cuffs gets back here, he meets a stone wall. A team. A team he ain't in no more. We play as a team, OK? And attack is the best form of defence.

THEO. *(to **MIKE** and **LIZ**)* We attack. You understand, you two?

BEBE. Now, Liz. You been close to Stacey. You're his collaborator, for Chrissake. Like Mike is mine. From this moment in time not any <u>more</u>, Liz, OK? We stick together – the three of us – it's <u>our</u> show he's killing, *(a beat)* That sonofabitch is gonna try to split us.

THEO. *(to the others)* Divide and conquer, you see, Mike? Liz?

BEBE. So we close ranks, right? Loyal. We're the three writers – music, lyrics, dialogue – we stay loyal. I'll spell it out for you...

LIZ. We're three writers, we can spell.

BEBE. <u>I</u> tell him what's wrong with the show – you support me. <u>You</u> tell him – vice versa.

THEO. *(to **MIKE** and **LIZ**)* Other way round, right?

BEBE. Liz? You understand?

(She looks at him, preoccupied with her own thoughts. Troubled. Torn.)

You understand, Liz?

LIZ. *(sadly)* Of course.

THEO. You agree?

LIZ. *(snapping)* Of course, Theo! Stop it!

THEO. Uh?

LIZ. Just stop it!

BEBE. OK, we are all agreed.

(A pause.)

(to **THEO***)* You want to hear *Long Time No See*, Latin American? Best thing I ever wrote. Best thing in the show. <u>Only</u> damn thing in the show. You wanna hear?

THEO. To tell you the honest truth, Bebe, I got a headache. Just recently I been getting these headaches.

BEBE. It'll <u>cure</u> it. No aspirin content whatever. I play piano – it cures <u>dandruff</u>.

*(***BEBE*** exits to SR wings. ***THEO*** wanders reluctantly after him.)*

(During the following **LIZ**/**MIKE** *dialogue* **BEBE** *plays – badly. He starts twice before finally playing the whole number through.)*

*(***MIKE*** and ***LIZ*** share a wry, resigned smile as ***BEBE*** starts playing.)*

MIKE. What time is it?

LIZ. *(checks watch)* Going on for quarter past six.

MIKE. What day is it?

LIZ. Thursday.

*(***MIKE*** gets his diary from his pocket. Studies one of the pages.)*

MIKE. "Thursday, six fifteen. Twenty-five lust-crazed petrol pump attendants from Potters Bar. Regent Palace Hotel. Orgy Suite. Will bring own oil."

(He puts the diary back in his pocket.)

Sod 'em! Let 'em wait!

*(**BEBE***'s second attempt is heard.)*

Do you think it works – going in Scene One?

LIZ. Mike. Do you know what I'd like to do?

*(End of **BEBE***'s second attempt.)*

MIKE. There isn't time, love. I've got these twenty-five lust-crazed petrol pump —

LIZ. I'd like to think about something else other than the show. I'd like to <u>talk</u> about something else. To <u>anybody</u>. To <u>feel</u> something about something else. Just once. Just for five minutes.

MIKE. Another eleven days, you <u>will</u>. It'll be over.

LIZ. It's like a disease. *(pause)* Jim's got this massive list of houses in Hampstead for me to see, when I've time. They're all marked off in order of preference. *(beat)* That's the worst of this disease: it's bloody contagious.

MIKE. Valerie won't talk about it at <u>all</u>. She says she doesn't want to tempt Providence.

LIZ. The worrying thing...the really worrying thing is... I can't think what else there <u>is</u>. To think about.

MIKE. There isn't <u>anything</u>. *(pause)* Well, that's if you don't count Poland.

*(The full version of "**LONG TIME NO SEE**" starts.)*

Kampuchea. Iran. Northern Ireland. The Middle East. Neo-Nazis. <u>Real</u> diseases. Deprived children. The loneliness of old age. Poverty. Despair. Death. *(beat)* And nineteen eighty-four — only two or three musicals away...

*(A silence – apart from **BEBE***'s stuttering rendition of *"**LONG TIME NO SEE**".)*

LIZ. It's all daft, isn't it?

MIKE. It's like Ealing in a way. Ealing isn't all glitter and tinsel. It's dog-eat-dog out there. *(beat)* What'll you do when you're a millionaire?

LIZ. Oh, I dunno. Start a waste-paper factory with all my rewrites. *(a beat: she grins)* I'll tell you the <u>first</u> thing I'll do. You know baked beans?

MIKE. *(blankly)* Do I know baked beans?

LIZ. Baked beans in a tin.

MIKE. Yes. I can safely say I do know baked beans in a tin...

LIZ. *(with growing enthusiasm)* Well. Whenever Jim fancies baked beans on toast – is this boring?

MIKE. Yes.

*(By this time, the rendering of "**LONG TIME NO SEE**" has finished.)*

LIZ. Well, whenever I open the tin – I always eat a spoonful <u>cold</u>. One spoonful. Before I put them in the pan. I can't resist cold baked beans out of the tin. So. When I'm a millionaire, the first thing I'll do is buy a whole tin, <u>large</u> – but not the really <u>big</u> large – that's sort of over the top, and eat the lot. Cold. Straight out of the tin.

(A pause.)

MIKE. Is that it?

LIZ. *(contentedly)* That's it.

MIKE. That turned out even more boring than I thought. Liz, I'll <u>buy</u> you a bloody tin! Tomorrow! You don't have to wait till you're —

LIZ. I do! I do! That's the whole point! It's <u>wasteful</u>. Till you've <u>earned</u> it! You've got to <u>earn</u> it...! *(a pause)* That isn't what I meant, really. I should've kept it to myself.

MIKE. You should. You should.

*(**STACEY** strides on from the wings, grim faced.)*

STACEY. Ok, let's start. The court will rise.

*(**MIKE** quickly stands up. **LIZ** also stands. A pause.)*

MIKE. *(shouts)* Theo! Stacey's here!

*(**BEBE** enters from the other side of the stage.)*

BEBE. *(to **LIZ**)* Loyal! L-O-Y-A-L. Loyal!

*(**THEO** slowly re-enters.)*

STACEY. Theo. You ready? 'Cause I'm <u>good</u> and ready! Let's go.

THEO. You fixed things with the designer?

STACEY. Thirteen scene changes, two days from previews, I don't fix in five minutes. Crap like this I fix in five minutes. Right – what's your problem?

THEO. We have some criticisms, Stacey.

STACEY. Of my direction.

THEO. Of your direction. Correct. We'd like them dealt with.

STACEY. OK, deal – then I'll deal.

THEO. OK, *(a pause)* Bebe, shoot!

BEBE. Stacey.

STACEY. Bebe.

BEBE. Act One, Scene One, page three —

STACEY. Gee! The first two pages are OK, then? Well, thank you, sir! Not as bad as I thought!

BEBE. On page three, the guy calls Maggie a "scheming bugger", right? Now me, I've only done twenty-eight Broadway hits, I never heard no one on stage say "bugger". You ever hear Fred Astaire call Ginger Rogers "bugger"? Me neither. "Bugger" is in bad taste, *(suddenly to **LIZ**)* Never write in bad taste. I don't know if it was your wrong time of the month or what – but bad taste is not necessary. West End audiences don't pay twenty bucks a head to hear "bugger". I want it out.

*(**LIZ** stares at **BEBE**, throughout, in total incredulity.)*

STACEY. Bebe...it's out. It's <u>already</u> out...

BEBE. I just want it out!

LIZ. It was cut <u>days</u> ago!! We're not here to talk about <u>lines</u>, <u>words</u> – you stupid old bugger – we're talking about <u>direction</u>!

BEBE. Hey! Hey! Now, just mind your lip, Miss goddamn Lizzie!

THEO. Liz, what the hell are you —

LIZ. We're here to talk about why whole <u>scenes</u> aren't working! Why we don't <u>cry</u> when we're <u>supposed</u> to cry! Why funny moments don't make us <u>laugh</u>! Why half of what we're saying is the opposite of what we <u>mean</u>! Why we're not telling the <u>story</u>! Why we don't know where to <u>look</u> when we <u>are</u>! Why what's supposed to be a West End show looks like Amateur Night Out on Southend Pier!

BEBE. *(aggressively)* Well, is that right?

LIZ. *(wearily)* That's right.

BEBE. Well, just you listen to <u>me</u>, gypsy! I cry when I'm supposed to cry. <u>My</u> tears are in my <u>music</u>. My music's <u>full</u> of tears, <u>and</u> laughter. You want a piece of boogie-woogie written – I write it eight tears to the bar!!

LIZ. "Boogie-woogie"?? *(to the others)* "Boogie-woogie"?? *(to* **BEBE***)* Bebe, there's no boogie-woogie in it!! That was nineteen-fifty – twenty-eight musicals ago!

BEBE. I'm giving you a for-instance! It's a for-instance! Where in hell don't you cry?

LIZ. In the show?

BEBE. Well, of <u>course</u> in the show!! What else are we talking about?!

LIZ. I don't cry anywhere. Where is it moving? Where is it touching?

BEBE. How about, Act One, Scene Five – the Maggie and Danny duet, *We Believe in Each Other.*

LIZ. Sentimental crap.

(A silence.)

BEBE. *(quietly, pondering)* What is it about the British? *(to* **STACEY***)* Can you tell me what it is about the British? *(to*

LIZ) They're buddies, for Chrissake! A bond between two <u>human</u> people, two buddies, is sentimental??

LIZ. It's a false emotion, Bebe. That means sentimental.

(He stares at her.)

BEBE. Loyalty is a false emotion – I ain't gone crazy??

LIZ. In your song – yes, Bebe! Because you've never felt the real thing in your life! <u>All</u> the things your songs are sentimental about – you don't actually give a <u>sod</u> for! Otherwise they <u>wouldn't</u> be – don't you see? Buddies. Loving Momma. The American flag. Apple pie. You feel sod-all for any of them. So you <u>pretend</u> to. Which is false.

(A pause.)

There are no tears of yours in your music, Bebe. There's <u>nothing</u> of you in your music.

(A pause.)

Have you noticed something? The one thing you're never sentimental about is <u>yourselves</u>.

*(The plural is not what **LIZ** meant to say. She glances quickly, troubled, at **STACEY** to see if he noticed she was including him in what she said.)*

*(She then looks back at **BEBE**.)*

LIZ. Your<u>self</u>.

BEBE. I <u>love</u> apple pie!

LIZ. When did you last eat it? Twenty-eight musicals ago?

THEO. Liz! *(turns on **MIKE**)* Mike! Please. The Board Operator will be going soon. We're supposed to be telling Stacey here —

*(**BEBE** is stony-faced)*

BEBE. I got nothing to tell him. Act One. Scene One. Page three. "Bugger". Everything else is a home run.

LIZ. How'd it go again? L-O-Y-A-L? Thanks, buddy!!

BEBE. He's doing a great job. I got no complaints.

(He clenches his jaw, clenches his fist and abruptly stalks off into the wings.)

*(**STACEY** sighs, smiles indulgently at the others.)*

STACEY. Listen, gang. Can I say something?

THEO. *(motioning him to carry on)* Stacey.

STACEY. First: one or two facts of life. OK, the show's a little rocky here and there, <u>seems</u> a little rocky. There are reasons – we're way behind schedule. New sets take time. Trying to get an English stage-crew to work like an American stage-crew takes time. Some of my priorities in direction have had to be sacrificed. But not any more. Now things change.

(A beat.)

Right, that's my intro. Now the message.

(A beat.)

Don't lose your nerve. You got a hundred notes for me, Mike. You got a hundred, Theo. Liz, you got <u>two</u> hundred, maybe. That's four hundred. <u>I</u> got <u>five</u> hundred. But what I <u>also</u> got – is <u>eleven</u> <u>whole</u> <u>days</u>. Don't lose-your-nerve.

(A beat.)

STACEY. We got nine previews – there'll be a real audience out there.

(Nods towards the auditorium.)

Real people. They'll laugh – or they won't. They'll cry – or they won't. And if they <u>don't</u> we'll <u>know</u> and we will fix it. And we'll do that nine times. The worst thing you can do at this moment in time is lose your nerve.

(A beat.)

You've lived with this goddamn show nearly a year – you can't <u>see</u> it no more! Like a...like you're trying to remember a dream...like a guy wearing contact lenses first time on.

(A beat.)

I <u>can</u> see it. Which is why I'm a director – and a good director. Which is why I can speak calmly and confidently...in the <u>certainty</u> that we got a hit.

(A beat.)

Which is why I know all your notes without hearing a single goddamn one of them. <u>I</u> got the same ones. And I'll fix them. Don't. Lose. Your. Nerve. Don't lose your nerve.

(A silence.)

THEO. Well, speaking as the Producer...

(He can't think of a thing to say. He peters away into silence.)

MIKE. Stacey... What time are we rehearsing tonight?

STACEY. Seven till however-long-it-takes.

*(**MIKE** looks at his watch.)*

MIKE. I'll see you at seven, then. I'm going to grab a sandwich. *(to **LIZ**)* Liz. Coming?

*(**LIZ** sits preoccupied. Doesn't answer.)*

*(He indicates 'cup of tea' to **THEO**.)*

Theo?

THEO. Cup of tea, good thinking.

*(**MIKE** exits.)*

Thank you, Stacey, for your...your contribution, after which – I'm sure I speak on behalf of all of us – I'm sure we all feel much more...um...

*(**THEO** starts to exit. Then turns to **STACEY**)*

Maybe I won't be here for tonight's rehearsal. I got some people to wine and dine. Investors. Potential investors. For when we take the show to Broadway. See you.

*(**THEO** exits.)*

(An uneasy embarrassed silence. Neither **LIZ** *nor* **STACEY** *look at each other.)*

LIZ. I'm sorry.

(He looks at her. She still avoids his eyes.)

I mean I'm sorry it had to be me to say all those things. <u>Somebody</u> had to.

STACEY. You used to think I was Superman.

LIZ. Yes. *(a beat)* A long time <u>ago</u>.

STACEY. So did I, a long time ago.

(She looks at him sharply, thrown by his first hint of self-doubt.)

I've still got eleven days to get it right.

LIZ. Or eleven days to <u>really</u> kill it.

STACEY. Do you have to go straight home after we finish tonight?

(She looks at him in puzzled amazement – and amusement.)

LIZ. Wow! How impetuous can you get! It's only taken you a year! You're sure you wouldn't like to <u>think</u> about it? I mean, every <u>other</u> decision you make takes you point three of a second, why not mull it over for <u>another</u> year or so? *(a beat)* Mind you, every other decision you make, you change.

STACEY. Do you? Have to go straight home?

LIZ. Yes. Well, no...but <u>yes</u>.

STACEY. Will you come back to the Hilton with me?

LIZ. No.

STACEY. I need to touch.

LIZ. I'm sorry.

STACEY. And <u>be</u> touched.

LIZ. I'm going straight home.

(She moves to exit but stops as **STACEY** *continues)*

STACEY. All this time...eight drafts, four weeks rehearsal, five weeks out of town, two weeks here...you <u>know</u> me.

LIZ. Stacey. I don't know you at <u>all</u>.

STACEY. You know my <u>work</u> – you know me.

LIZ. Exactly. I look at the show and I see nothing. A blur. I see fragments of things that nearly make sense...<u>nearly</u>. I see a mess. A glossy mess – but never anything inside. I don't see <u>you</u> at <u>all</u>.

(She looks at him.)

Or perhaps that <u>is</u> seeing you. *(a beat)* Your <u>clothes</u> are beautiful.

(A pause.)

STACEY. I'm going to say something...

LIZ. Don't. Don't say any more.

STACEY. I'm going to say it once. Then I want you to forget I ever said it at <u>all</u>. If you <u>don't</u> – then the show really is in trouble.

LIZ. *(puzzled)* What?

STACEY. If you forget it, then <u>I</u> will. And that means it'll never have been said.

LIZ. *(perplexed)* Why say it then?

STACEY. Because then you'll know me. *(a beat)* As opposed to what I said before, the show <u>is</u> one hell of a mess. And by saying it's like Southend Pier, you insult Southend Pier.

(A pause.)

STACEY. I don't know <u>how</u> to make it right, Liz. I don't think I ever <u>did</u>, even at the start. Terrific.

(A beat.)

It's a musical – there's no right way, no wrong way. Something happens or it doesn't. And on this show, it <u>hasn't</u>. Something won't gel: I don't even know <u>what</u>, let alone how to <u>make</u> it. I'm lost.

(A beat.)

LIZ. Some of it's...um...good. The street scene with the car horns integrated into the music. It's never been done before.

STACEY. George Gershwin. *An American in Paris.*

(A beat.)

So, what do you do if you're lost, Liz? Well, if you're British, strikes me you beef about it, give up and drown. If you're an American, you eat a little apple pie, you think of Momma back home, you salute the Stars and Stripes and you stay <u>loyal</u>. To your<u>self</u>. And you do it <u>singing</u>. You may still drown. On the other hand, someone may hear you. And <u>save</u> you.

LIZ. Who?

STACEY. You sing loud enough, everyone <u>applauds</u>. The <u>audience</u> saves you.

(A pause.)

Will you come back with me tonight?

(A pause. He smiles.)

I'd appreciate an answer in point three of a second.

LIZ. Even the <u>wrong</u> one? Sorry, Stacey. That ship has sailed.

STACEY. *(briskly, confidently)* OK, all that you forget. None of it was said. The following you <u>remember</u>... Trust me. This show is a hit. We'll fix it. As I do believe our producer has mentioned – we got here absolutely the best team, working together, having fun —

(He stops as he, and we, hear a violent commotion offstage.)

*(He and **LIZ** look towards the wings, puzzled.)*

BEBE. *(offstage)* Yeah? Well, she takes it back – stuck-up frigid bitch – her first show and <u>she</u> tells me —

THEO. *(offstage)* Bebe! Don't be a schmock – what good does it do —

(**BEBE** *storms ferociously in, brusquely handing off* **MIKE** *and* **THEO** *as they try to restrain him.*)

BEBE. She apologises, apologises – or I'm off the show – I withdraw my music —

MIKE. Bebe, we're all a bit edgy at the moment —

BEBE. On her goddamn knees she apologises.

THEO. Bebe, please!

(**BEBE** *storms up to* **LIZ**)

BEBE. OK, baby! You think my music stinks, right?

LIZ. Bebe, go away, I'm tired.

(*He pushes her shoulder, hard.*)

BEBE. Yeah, well, you give me the respect due, OK?! You know who I am, you frigid gypsy bitch?

(*He pokes her in the chest as he talks.*)

LIZ. Don't poke like that, Bebe.

(**LIZ** *backs away.*)

(**BEBE** *continues poking at her.*)

BEBE. You know my music is too goddamn good for your lousy book – you know that?!

STACEY. Bebe, cool it.

(**BEBE** *pokes* **LIZ** *in the chest again.*)

BEBE. Huh? Huh?

LIZ. Bebe – don't poke.

BEBE. You're a tight-assed broad, you know <u>that</u>?!

(*He pokes her again.*)

LIZ. (*yelling*) Bebe – don't poke!!

(*She pushes his arm away, violently. He promptly punches her in the face.*)

THEO. Jesus!

(THEO attempts to pull BEBE off LIZ as they begin wrestling and raining blows on each other. BEBE pushes THEO away. THEO falls over.)

(MIKE rushes in to part them.)

STACEY. Mike! Get the hell out of it!

MIKE. He's punching a <u>woman</u> for God's sake!

(STACEY tries to pull MIKE away. MIKE makes a grab for STACEY. They grapple and fall to the floor.)

(Suddenly all the lights go out.)

(In the darkness, LIZ takes a kick at BEBE.)

(He screams in pain.)

BEBE. She's just kicked me in the —

(The BOARD OPERATOR calmly enters, and crosses the stage)

BOARD OP. Six-thirty! Good night!

Scene Two

(The manager's office, St. James Theatre.)

(About 10 p.m. on the opening night of the musical. Summer.)

(The room is festive with bouquets of flowers and telegrams. On the desk is a row of five bottles of champagne.)

*(We can hear a musical number begin: "**THE NEXT TRAIN TO HEAVEN**". About 20 seconds later, LIZ comes in. She's looking radiant in a stunning evening dress. She's agitated, excited, and shaking with happiness.)*

*(**LIZ** makes her way excitedly to the middle of the room – then stops stock-still. She then sits down and immediately stands up again. We hear applause for the number.)*

LIZ. Oh, God! Oh, my God!

*(**MIKE** bursts in. He's wearing a tuxedo.)*

MIKE. Are you alright, Liz?

LIZ. Listen to the applause, Mike!

MIKE. Why are you pacing the back of the circle like a pregnant usherette —

LIZ. Oh, God, just listen to them!

*(Through the applause, "**THE PEOPLE ARE ONLY HUMAN**" Tap number begins.)*

*(**MIKE** grins at **LIZ**. She grins back. A moment of massive relief between them.)*

MIKE. *(quietly)* A hit, do you think?

LIZ. *(quietly)* A smash.

MIKE. *(quietly)* A smasheroo! *(a beat)* Liz, come back in. You've lived with it for a bloody year – you can last another two minutes!

(The applause has died down. MIKE listens to the music for a moment.)

MIKE. Helen's dance. *(a beat)* Come and stand at the back.

(We hear applause during the number.)

(LIZ turns to MIKE, heart pounding.)

LIZ. They're even applauding in the <u>middle</u>...!

MIKE. Listen, the mood <u>they're</u> in, you could go out there and play the Peruvian National Anthem on <u>spoons</u> and they'd applaud.

LIZ. I can't bear to watch.

(She wanders over to the desk.)

I'll stay here and drink champagne.

*(Through the applause, we hear the finale, "**WHATEVER HAPPENED TO TOMORROW?**" starting.)*

(LIZ looks at the bottles of champagne.)

Only five bottles? Aren't you lot having any?

(The applause has died down and MIKE realises it is the last number.)

MIKE. Christ – they've started the finale!

(They both stand and listen for a moment.)

(LIZ cradling a bottle of champagne is quieter, calmer, still.)

LIZ. The finale. Finally, finally...the finale,

(MIKE can stand it no longer.)

MIKE. I gotta see this.

(He races out. LIZ still stands, quietly singing along, then she too races out.)

(After about 10 seconds, we hear the tremendous applause from the auditorium.)

(MIKE and LIZ come rushing back in.)

MIKE. They're standing! They're actually <u>standing</u>!

(He runs to the desk and starts opening a bottle of champagne.)

Someone actually shouted "bravo". Probably my mother. Or my agent. *(to the bottle)* Keep still, will you? That's all I need – a nervous bottle...

*(***STACEY*** comes bounding in. Like **LIZ** when she first entered, he's almost beside himself with relief and joy.)*

*(***MIKE*** succeeds in opening the bottle of champagne and starts pouring it out.)*

STACEY. Can you hear 'em?

LIZ. I can hear 'em. I can hear 'em.

STACEY. They don't write songs like that any more

(They laugh.)

I've got time for one drink then I'll go backstage and see the cast – stroke the donkeys' noses.

(They stand, glasses in hand, listening to the tremendous gales of enthusiastic applause. They realise that the finale is about to end.)

STACEY. Hey, we can't miss the curtain calls!

(All three rush out.)

(As the finale ends, we see the lights from the theatre going up and down for the curtain calls.)

*(The calls end, and **LIZ**, **STACEY** and **MIKE** return. Pick up their glasses of champagne.)*

STACEY. I was right about Annabel!

LIZ. You were right about everything!

MIKE. I'll trust you the rest of my life!

*(***THEO*** comes bounding in. Sees the others drinking champagne and tries to look like a calm, blasé producer who happens to have a hit on his hands. He leans on the filing cabinet.)*

THEO. Very nice. You don't wait for your producer? Where'd you learn your manners? The Royal Shakespeare Company?

LIZ. Theo, they love it! They love it! I love it!

*(**THEO** is almost shaking with excitement and relief. He tries even harder to hide it.)*

THEO. I been a producer since I was six years old. I never heard an audience like that.

(Suddenly he can control his feelings no longer.)

We got a goddamn <u>hit</u>!!!

MIKE. Oh hell, really? Just when everything was going so well...

*(He takes a glass of champagne to **THEO**.)*

STACEY. And the show ain't bad.

*(**LIZ** turns to him. Smiles. Goes over to him.)*

LIZ. *(quietly)* Not bad at all, Stacey.

*(**STACEY** grins, shrugs.)*

STACEY. So we did a little potchkeying here and there...a bit of this, a bit of that...

*(**LIZ** kisses him, tenderly, unhurriedly.)*

THEO. Ahem, ahem.

*(**LIZ** turns to **THEO**.)*

Well, speaking as the producer...speaking as the producer – I can't think of a damn thing to say!

(They all laugh contentedly, quietly.)

(The applause has finally died away.)

MIKE. *(to **LIZ**)* Jim's taking Valerie to the shindig, right?

LIZ. Yes. We meet them there.

MIKE. Was he enjoying it?

LIZ. When I was pacing the stalls, he kept turning round and giving me a thumbs-up sign. He was sitting with his programme in one hand and his list of Hampstead houses in the other. Did Valerie like it?

MIKE. I think so.

STACEY. Think? Wasn't she facing the stage?

MIKE. Well, halfway through the applause for the duet —

THEO. And <u>what</u> applause, eh? Hands clapping and clapping like those things taking wing...the things that take wing...<u>flamingoes</u>...things that take wing.

MIKE. Well, halfway through the applause, she turned to me and whispered "I think Raymond needs glasses".

THEO. Raymond? Who the hell's Raymond?

MIKE. Our youngest. Raymond. The punk one. He was seven in April.

LIZ. Hey! She's started talking about the kids again? Instead of lyrics? Tonight of all nights?

MIKE. To be honest, what she actually said was, "I think Raymond needs glasses/He screws up his eyes/He'll look very wise/For a kid of his size". *(a beat)* A, b, b, b.

(A little kind laughter from the others. **BEBE** *then walks in. He's wearing a tuxedo. Once again, he walks in without actually looking at anyone.)*

BEBE. You want the manager's office, you gotta ask ten times. No one speaks English round here. I went to tell the orchestra they did OK. They ain't Americans, they did OK! Tomorrow they'll be better.

MIKE. Bebe! Champagne!

BEBE. You got any plain water back there?

THEO. You want <u>water</u>, Maestro??

BEBE. I <u>like</u> water.

MIKE. Water it is!

(He starts pouring a glass of water from a jug.)

*(***STACEY*** smiles contentedly at* **BEBE**.*)*

STACEY. Well, kiddo? It was ecstasy-time out there! Right?

BEBE. *(to* **LIZ***)* Hey, you were right about the gag when he gives her the letter. Great gag. Biggest laugh in the show.

LIZ. Thanks, Bebe.

BEBE. You're welcome. How many times have I given you a compliment?

LIZ. That's true.

BEBE. Listen, you do a show – you do a show. We take this one to Broadway, it'll be my twenty-ninth. I don't know if you ever knew that. *(a beat)* All the screaming and hollering – that's our way of saying "please". We say <u>nothing</u> – that means "thank you".

(A pause.)

Hey! I almost forgot!

(He takes a box from his breast-pocket. Hands it to **LIZ***.)*

Liz. Thank you.

LIZ. Oh, Bebe!

(She opens it. Takes out a gold chain.)

Bebe, it's gorgeous. Thank <u>you</u>.

BEBE. You're welcome, *(to* **THEO***)* And thanks for the watch.

THEO. You're welcome.

LIZ. *(to* **THEO***)* And for mine.

THEO. My pleasure.

MIKE. *(to* **THEO***)* And for mine.

THEO. Listen, you did nice "moons" and "Junes", enjoy it. The least I could do.

STACEY. Hey! A toast!

LIZ. I think I'll buy myself a tin of baked beans in the morning...

STACEY. I'd like to propose a toast.

(He raises his glass.)

THEO. Baked beans on toast!

(They all laugh. And drink. Except **BEBE***.)*

LIZ. You OK, Bebe? Tired?

BEBE. Tired? You ever seen me be tired? I'm older than all of you. <u>Twice</u> as old as all of you. All of you put together.

(A pause.)

Listen, I just done another show – that makes me six thousand years old. The curtain comes down – I'm allowed to be tired.

(An emotional silence.)

LIZ. Hey fellas, guess what! I'm crying! Unless one of you is peeling onions!

*(***THEO*** hands her his handkerchief.)*

THEO. Gentlemen – <u>lady</u> and gentlemen – if everybody's gonna start crying all over the place, I think it's a blessing I make a little speech. Don't worry, not a <u>big</u> little speech, just a <u>little</u> little speech. *(a beat)* Team, we did it. We <u>made</u> it. And I just want to say thank you. Thank you from the bottom of my heart – which some of you didn't even think I had! We're going to run five years, six, maybe ten. Eat your heart out, *Evita*! *(a beat)* So we go out there now, collect our loved ones, the investors.

(They all laugh.)

I don't mean...I mean <u>and</u> the investors, and the cast and everybody. We go to our party – compliments of your producer. We have a night to remember. Tomorrow morning at ten – I give you the chance of a lie-in, after all these months you're entitled – tomorrow at ten you join me in my hotel suite for breakfast. Maybe I get Stacey a jumbo prawn cocktail, special delivery. We eat breakfast, read the reviews, discuss mounting the show for Broadway, <u>then</u>...well, then, nothing. Your day's your own. You can watch them change the whatisits at Buckingham Palace —

LIZ. Sheets!

THEO. *(laughing)* Sheets! Whatever. *(a beat)* Lady and gentlemen, thank you for making me happy. And <u>rich</u>. But, most of all – believe it or not – for making me – rich!!

(They all nurse their glasses, and their emotions, in silence.)

LIZ. Quiet now. No more clapping. Well, just a bit.

*(She looks at **BEBE** and starts clapping him. The others all, except **BEBE**, join in clapping one another.)*

THEO. OK, let's go backstage now and say thank you to our cast.

(THEO, STACEY, MIKE *and* **LIZ** *start to exit, leaving* **BEBE** *sitting alone.)*

LIZ. *(exiting)* What for? What have <u>they</u> done?

Scene Three

(A suite in a London hotel. The morning after the night before.)

(The curtains are drawn closed but a chink of early morning light filters through.)

*(**LIZ**, wearing **THEO**'s tuxedo over her evening dress, is fast asleep on the sofa.)*

*(**BEBE** is fast asleep in a chair – which is in the same relative position as the one he occupied in the Manager's Office.)*

*(**STACEY** is asleep on the floor R.)*

(The room bears the debris of a late-night party. A couple of champagne bottles lie empty, one with a rose in. There are dirty ashtrays, glasses and coffee cups lying around. A large empty coffee-pot and dirty cups are on a tray on the floor.)

(Shoes are off, ties are undone.)

*(There's a faint sound of intermittent snoring. And a little incoherent rambling in his sleep from **BEBE**.)*

*(The light in the lift UR comes on. The door opens and a **WAITER** enters with a breakfast trolley.)*

(He pushes the trolley to the C of the room. He gently knocks on the top of the trolley. No one wakes.)

(He knocks on the trolley again, not quite so gently. Again, no one wakes.)

(He crosses to the side table UL and knocks even louder.)

THEO. *(offstage)* OK! OK!

(The bedroom light (offstage) is switched on.)

I ever do a show with a lot of goddamn knocking in, you got the part!

(A pause.)

*(**THEO** trundles in from the bedroom. He's wearing dishevelled pyjamas and struggling to do up his dressing gown.)*

(As he enters, he reacts in slightly hungover distaste to the stale air in the room. He glances at the sleeping bodies.)

WAITER. Room service, sir. Good morning.

THEO. Uh?

WAITER. You ordered breakfast for five.

THEO. It's morning?

WAITER. Pardon?

THEO. What time in the morning?

WAITER. Ten-fifteen, sir. You <u>ordered</u> it for ten-fifteen. *(a beat)* Well, ten o'clock.

*(**THEO** crosses UR to the window curtain pulley. He opens the curtains and daylight streams into the room.)*

THEO. You got the papers?

WAITER. Yes, sir.

THEO. You got all the daily papers?

WAITER. All here, sir.

THEO. I told the Hall goddamn Porter I had to have all the daily papers, priority.

WAITER. Yes, sir. These are they, sir.

*(He hands the thick bundle of newspapers to **THEO**, who holds them to his chest as he crosses to the UL table and turns the cassette deck on. "**EVERYTHING'S COMING UP ROSES**" by Ethel Merman blares out.)*

*(**LIZ** suddenly sits upright, and the light and the noise have also woken **STACEY** and **BEBE**.)*

THEO. Come on you guys. You know what time it is? We got the papers!

(**THEO** *drops a couple of papers in front of* **LIZ**, *one for* **BEBE**, *takes one himself and puts the rest on the floor near* **STACEY**.)

STACEY. Any coffee there?

WAITER. Coffee for five, sir.

THEO. Stacey. Papers. Read.

BEBE. Someone mention coffee?

WAITER. Coffee for five, sir.

(**BEBE** *wanders over to the trolley and starts pouring a cup of coffee*.)

(*The phone rings.* **STACEY** *levers himself up and goes towards it*.)

THEO. Is it for me?

STACEY. *(to the ringing phone)* Are you for him? *(the phone stops its ring) (to* **THEO***)* No reply. *(to the phone)* I asked you a question. *(the phone rings again)*

THEO. Stacey, for Chrissakes, I got middle-aged knees – once they're bent, they ain't open to discussion!

(**STACEY** *has answered the phone*.)

STACEY. *(into phone)* Yeah? *(pause)* No, but he ain't a million miles away. Hang on. *(to* **THEO***)* It is for you, Theo-baby.

(**THEO** *heaves himself up and grabs the phone*.)

THEO. *(into phone)* Hello? *(pause, then urgently)* Yep! Wait, I'll get a pencil! *(to* **STACEY***)* Stacey, you got a pencil?

STACEY. I gave you a twenty-two-carat gold pen for opening night! Engraved yet!

THEO. I'm in my dressing gown for chrissake!

(*The* **WAITER** *coughs embarassedly*.)

(into phone) OK, go ahead!

(*During the above sequence,* **LIZ** *has wakened, looked around to get her bearings, registered what's happening, and crawled off the settee to the newspapers on the floor*.)

(**STACEY** *walks past* **LIZ** *on his way upstage to turn off the cassette player.*)

STACEY. *(not looking at her)* Morning.

LIZ. *(not looking at him)* Morning.

(**BEBE** *crosses to the window. Stands looking out, sipping his coffee.*)

THEO. *(into phone)* Yeah. Go on.

(*He writes on a writing pad as he listens.*)

(**LIZ** *has found the first review.*)

(*As* **STACEY** *switches off the cassette, she rises slowly to her feet reading it – in horror and disbelief.*)

LIZ. Oh, my God...!

(**THEO, BEBE** *and* **STACEY** *jerk their eyes towards her, anxiously. She continues reading (the Guardian) with an increasingly sinking heart.*)

WAITER. *(to* **THEO***)* Will there be anything further, sir?

(**THEO** *ignores him.*)

LIZ. He hated it.

(**THEO, BEBE** *and* **STACEY** *stare at her.*)

WAITER. *(to* **THEO***)* I take it everything is to your satisfaction, sir?

LIZ. The audience loved it. He hated it.

(*She turns and looks at them, blankly.*)

THEO. *(quietly, in quiet dread)* What's it say?

LIZ. The headline is "Kiss Tomorrow Goodbye".

WAITER. *(to* **THEO***)* If all is in order, then, sir...

THEO. Read it, Liz.

LIZ. *(reading)* "*Whatever Happened to Tomorrow?* St. James Theatre...many musicals spring happily from the wombs of successful novels. This one struggles half-heartedly out, untunefully yelping – and falls flat on its face."

(**STACEY** *begins to read out the review from his first paper (the* Telegraph*)*)

STACEY. *(reading)* "Last night I saw the best argument yet put forward for turning our theatres into car-parks and staying in to watch the telly... A tasteless, artificial musical which..."

(He looks at the others in bewilderment.)

I don't believe it...

(None too pleased at the absence of a tip, the **WAITER** *crosses to the lift and enters. The lift light going out indicates the departure of the lift. They have all ignored him.)*

THEO. *(into phone)* Yeah, yeah, OK, I get the gist. What about the others?

*(***BEBE** *sits impassively drinking his coffee.)*

*(***LIZ** *throws aside the next paper (*The Sun*) she's been skimming through.)*

LIZ. Nothing at all in this one...

(Meanwhile, **STACEY** *has found the next review (the* Financial Times*))*

STACEY. Hey! A good one! I think we got a good one! He reads from the paper.

(reading) "An interesting evening...blah, blah, blah... Various passable performances from a competent cast...blah, blah, blah...not well-enough staged to retain one's interest."

(To the others, incredulously)

Who is this creep? He just said it was an interesting evening!

(Resumes reading)

"...songs stuck in sentimental syrup...a lazily-written book..."

LIZ. "Lazily"? Not "<u>lazily</u>"?

STACEY. *(reading)* "...gossip has it that both director and composer threatened to resign from the show before it even went into rehearsal. After seeing the show, I can only assume they actually <u>did</u>."

LIZ. I thought you said that one was a good one?

STACEY. *(reading)* "*Whatever Happened to Tomorrow?* – better you don't ask."

*(He throws the paper aside and starts flicking through the next one. (*The Mail*))*

THEO. *(into phone)* Well, of <u>course</u> I'm listening, you dumb cluck! Some smart-ass condemns me to death, I tend to listen.

*(**LIZ** finds the next review, (*The Times*))*

LIZ. *(reading)* "*Whatever Happened to Tomorrow?* Whatever happened to good musicals?"

BEBE. Something always told me that title was <u>asking</u> for trouble...

*(**STACEY** finds the review he has been looking for in the next paper)*

STACEY. *(excitedly)* "Nicely written, nicely scored... "

(To the others.)

Hey! We got a fan!

(resumes reading)

"...nicely acted, sung, danced and directed... Unfortunately, niceness isn't enough to..."

(He throws the newspaper down.)

THEO. *(into phone)* Debra! Do me a favour, let me do the sighing!

*(**LIZ** has meanwhile, emptily, disinterestedly almost, found the review in the last paper (the Express).)*

LIZ. *(reading)* "*Whatever Happened to Tomorrow?* a new musical, was given an ecstatic reception by its glittering first-night audience at the St. James Theatre..."

(to the others)

At least he was <u>there</u>!!

(Resumes reading)

(reading) "...by its glittering first-night audience at the St. James Theatre. Unfortunately, first-night audiences are notoriously unable to distinguish between..."

(The light in the lift comes on and the door opens and **MIKE** *enters – carrying a stack of morning papers. He is as pale and heavy-hearted as the others, and is in time to hear:)*

Oh, Jesus,

(She sighs and throws aside the newspaper.)

MIKE. Sorry I'm late. *(a pause)* You've seen them then.

STACEY. *(numbly)* We've seen them.

MIKE. Morning, all.

(They all ignore him. A silence.)

(to **STACEY***)* You look as though you've been up all night.

STACEY. Theo turned in about four a.m. We kept going till five, five thirty.

LIZ. *(numbly)* Laughing. Doing a lot of laughing.

(A silence)

MIKE. Barmy. All of you. We were in bed by two. These – *(he indicates his newspapers)* – came at seven. At least I got five hours' kip. Bloody good job I did – with this lot waiting on the doorstep. *(He sighs)* Unbelievable, isn't it?

(No one replies.)

It's just unbelievable. *(He turns to* **LIZ***)* Are you alright, Liz?

(She nods, very near to tears.)

MIKE. Jim enjoy the party?

LIZ. I think so. We had a row. He wanted me to go home – I wanted to come on here. He was right, as usual. At least we could've read these <u>together.</u>

(During this sequence, **MIKE** *has sat on the sofa.)*

THEO. *(into phone, gravely)* Thank you, Debra... *(pause)* No, no...no more. Enough's enough.

(He replaces the phone. Looks at the others with dead eyes.)

(Reading from his notes) New Evening Standard, bad to middling, We needed the *New Evening Standard*. People read it on the subway...they got nothing else to do... *(he sighs) The Sunday Times* gave it six lines – or, rather, will be <u>giving</u> it six lines...

MIKE. How the hell have you got that?

THEO. Spies. I got friends in Fleet Street.

(He glances at his written notes. Sighs.)

Not as many as I'd like.

(He reads from his notes.)

"The St. James Theatre, in its wisdom, has seven pillars supporting the circle. As luck would have it, I was not behind any one of them..."

STACEY. I make it three lousy, two not too bad, one OK.

*(**LIZ** is staring at **STACEY**.)*

LIZ. "One OK"? Am I deaf? Which is the "one OK"?

STACEY. Listen, a little judicious editing, we got some good quotes even in the bad ones...

(He motions towards the papers)

"An ecstatic audience reception" someone said, somewhere in there. We got enough for front-of-house quotes. We did OK.

LIZ. Stacey! Have you gone bloody bananas! We did terrible.

THEO. So. That's six lousy, one not too bad, one sort of OK.

(He looks round at them, almost in tears.)

That's the way it goes, folks.

(A heavy-hearted silence.)

So, who'd have thought it, my children? We got ourselves a flop.

(A small pause.)

BEBE. Me. <u>I'd</u> have thought it. I knew in Manchester

THEO. With hindsight, we <u>all</u> knew in Manchester.

BEBE. And I knew for certain last night.

LIZ. The audience <u>loved</u> it, Bebe.

BEBE. I knew just the same. Who takes notice of audiences? <u>We're</u> the ones who know, *(a beat)* Not <u>know</u> exactly. <u>Feel</u>. My bones felt it. <u>They</u> knew.

(He sits down at the writing desk.)

LIZ. I didn't want to live in Hampstead anyway. It's full of bloody writers.

STACEY. *(to* **THEO***)* What's the advance bookings?

THEO. Ten thousands pounds.

LIZ. Well, that's marvellous. Isn't it?

THEO. Enough to keep us running for three nights.

*(***STACEY*** briskly gathers his thoughts.)*

STACEY. OK. So. The position is this. Good quotes front-of-house. After last night's audience – terrific word-of-mouth. A little advance booking. OK. *(a beat)*

*(***STACEY*** rises)*

So, <u>now</u> what we do Theo is we advertise. We saturate Theo, <u>saturate</u>! The newspapers – specially those who knifed us. TV. Hoardings. Subways...

THEO. Stacey. Stacey-baby. We ain't got no money to advertise.

*(***STACEY*** stares at him, apprehensively.)*

STACEY. I'm talking about fifty thousand. Nothing big.

THEO. There's nothing.

(They all stare at him, incredulously.)

(A pause.)

STACEY. Nothing??

THEO. That ship has sunk, Stacey. *(a beat)* I'm two hundred thousand dollars in debt.

(A horrified silence.)

(He smiles at them, bleakly.)

And I'll tell you a little joke. A <u>sick</u> joke, eh? It's my birthday today. The 26th of June. Anyone feel like singing?

STACEY. Theo. *(quietly, incredulously)* You're how much in debt?

THEO. *(turning on him angrily)* You changed the costumes. You wanted me to scrap the sets. Eighty thousand pounds. I scrapped them. You change a number, the music has to be re-copied. You change it again – it has to be re-copied again. It has to be rehearsed, and re-rehearsed, with a twenty-piece orchestra, all on overtime.

(A beat.)

(quietly) Also, one or two of the investors didn't honour their pledges.

BEBE. What?

THEO. One gentleman in particular. *(a beat)* Is it my fault not everyone's a gentleman?

(a beat)

We went into rehearsal forty-thousand pounds under-capitalised. I didn't say nothing. You had enough to worry about. You were my team...absolutely the best goddamn team in the...

(a beat)

It all depended on one thing. Reviews.

(a beat)

With the team I got. Absolutely the best team in the goddamn world. And it brought me in a flop. A whatsit flop. Definite!

(A silence)

BEBE. It wasn't a bad little show. It wasn't the greatest either. Maybe we shoulda stayed with the first draft – who knew?

(LIZ *silently raises her hand.)*

Plus you got from me maybe not-so-hot a score I'd have done from a better book, maybe. The lyrics? Well, I seen better lyrics on a Jewish Christmas card. Plus we got arguably the messiest direction in the history of mess. We killed <u>ourselves</u>.

(A silence.)

LIZ. A whole year... I'd formed a company to save on tax. It cost me more than my advance...

THEO. Everyone, I'd like to ask a favour. A favour I never believed was going to be necessary. But it is. *(a beat)* I don't think the show will run a month.

BEBE. Six weeks, tops.

THEO. Six weeks! I'll be even <u>more</u> in debt! I'll sell my house, of course. It won't be enough. It ain't Buckingham Palace! *(a beat)* I'd like to ask you all – officially – to forego your royalties. You'll hardly notice but it may help a little with my debts.

(STACEY, **BEBE**, **MIKE** *and* **LIZ** *all nod their agreement.)*

I'm sorry to have to ask you. I'm embarrassed. I apologise.

(A silence.)

Thank you. All of you.

(THEO *crosses to the trolley.)*

Anyone like some breakfast? I got tea, coffee, black, white, toast, eggs and bacon. Liz –

*(**THEO** uncovers an ice bucket on the trolley and lifts out a large tin of –)*

Baked beans – all cold.

(A pause.)

(He looks round the debris of the room.)

THEO. Maybe we clean up the joint a little, huh? Clear a little of the garbage away...

*(**THEO**, **LIZ** and **MIKE** start clearing papers off the floor.)*

BEBE. *(to **THEO**)* So. When do we start work on the Broadway show?

*(**LIZ** stands, with a bundle of papers in her arms.)*

(She stares at him as though he's gone mad.)

LIZ. What Broadway show??

BEBE. This Broadway show!

LIZ. What??

BEBE. We got everything to do. New script, right? A new score – well, maybe <u>half</u> a new score – a lot of them tunes are the best goddamn tunes I ever wrote!

STACEY. *(briskly)* The first things we fix are the production schedules. We're now June twenty-sixth, right?

THEO. Right!

BEBE. Right!

STACEY. Right!

LIZ. Right??

STACEY. So, if we work backwards from the proposed opening date –

*(**LIZ** is staring at **THEO**)*

LIZ. Did you say "right"?

THEO. Right!

LIZ. "Right"? You're two hundred thousand dollars in debt! How can you do another show?

THEO. You do another show, you pay off your debts.

LIZ. <u>How</u>??

(A beat)

THEO. Easy! You make it a <u>hit</u>!

STACEY. *(to* **BEBE** *and* **THEO***)* So, if we aim to open Broadway, March, April...

THEO. I'd be happier with February...the show's already in good shape...

LIZ. *(yelling)* I don't believe it!!

(They all turn and look at her.)

We've got a flop – and you're talking about Broadway! What for? <u>Another</u>? Can't you <u>read</u>?

(She throws her armful of newspapers at them. They scatter on the floor.)

(A pause.)

THEO. Well, of <u>course</u> we're talking about Broadway, you horse's ass! We'll do six years on Broadway <u>minimum</u>. Then we do the movie. You got a piece of the movie rights – you'll make a quarter of a million! <u>Also</u> minimum.

BEBE. <u>Half</u> a million. *(to* **THEO***)* You talking pounds or dollars?

STACEY. *(gently)* Liz. We were <u>always</u> going to Broadway. This is just the beginning.

*(**THEO**, **BEBE** and **STACEY** pull up three chairs by the writing desk, consulting their diaries.)*

*(**LIZ** stands, **MIKE** seated, watch them.)*

THEO. Now, I'm back in New York July ninth. You go back Friday, Bebe, am I right? You, too Stacey.

STACEY. Friday, Saturday, whenever. So, assuming draft one's written by mid-July...

BEBE. And me and Mike get one or two ideas for a coupla songs...

THEO. I'll call *Variety*. Maybe this time they spell my name right!

MIKE. Hello, Liz.

LIZ. Hello, Mike.

MIKE. What's a year between friends?

BEBE. I'll call New York. The Schuberts'll take anything of mine.

(**LIZ** *looks at* **MIKE**, *smiles, and sits next to him on the sofa.*)

LIZ. Do you know something, young man?

MIKE. Less and less with every show!

LIZ. You never propositioned me. The only one who didn't.

MIKE. I knew I'd forgotten <u>something</u>...

LIZ. We could have had an affair.

MIKE. Yes, we could.

STACEY. I got a notion. For the States, we change the social worker to an analyst!

THEO. Yeah. And maybe, we could change the GI bride to a Cuban refugee...

BEBE. For the States, we get an American co-writer – no disrespect to the broad.

(**LIZ** *and* **MIKE** *smile at each other.*)

MIKE. We still could have an affair.

LIZ. Too late now, Mike. It's the morning after.

MIKE. So we won't.

LIZ. Suppose not.

MIKE. Why?

BEBE. *(rising)* We can't miss on Broadway. We'll make it an all-black show!!!

LIZ. You know what they say: never carry your fantasies into real life. *(a beat)* My New Zealand rugby forwards would've knocked hell out of you.

MIKE. My black lesbians would've scratched your eyes out.

(*A small pause.*)

LIZ. *(smiles)* Still. It was nice being married to you just the same.

MIKE. <u>Very</u> nice.

(They kiss, then part. As friends.)

STACEY. Liz? Can you have a new first draft ready by mid-July? You got three whole weeks...

BEBE. Mike? I'll need you in New York, July twentieth, OK?

*(**MIKE** nods agreement.)*

THEO. And in the meantime – as producer – I'll start setting up the —

LIZ. *(rising)* Excuse me, gentlemen! I've got an idea.

THEO. Listen. Any ideas, at the right <u>time</u>, Liz, are always whatisit, but right now we're in the middle of —

LIZ. I'd like to suggest that we all form a circle and take our clothes off —

BEBE. What?

STACEY. What's she say?

LIZ. We all get in a circle with no clothes on...

THEO. Liz! We're discussing the Broadway production!

LIZ. We all get into a circle with no clothes on...and we fuck each other.

(A very long silence as they all stare at her in total incomprehension.)

THEO. Liz! We're supposed to be discussing <u>Broadway</u>!

(She smiles at him, sadly.)

LIZ. Theo. I am.

(Curtain)

Lightning Source UK Ltd.
Milton Keynes UK
UKOW03f1009010913

216267UK00001B/3/P